# GROWING
# CACTI
## AND OTHER
# SUCCULENTS
## IN THE
# CONSERVATORY
## AND
# INDOORS

# GROWING

# CACTI

## AND OTHER

# SUCCULENTS

## IN THE

# CONSERVATORY

## AND

# INDOORS

## SHIRLEY-ANNE BELL

First published 2001 by
Guild of Master Craftsman Publications Ltd,
166 High Street, Lewes,
East Sussex BN7 1XU
Copyright © GMC Publications Ltd 2001
Text © Shirley-Anne Bell 2001
Drawings © Shirley-Anne Bell 2001

ISBN 1 86108 205 3

A catalogue record of this book is available from the British Library.

Editor: David Arscott
Designer: Jane Hawkins
Photographer: Neville Bell
Cover photograph: © Vale Garden Houses, Harlaxton, Lincolnshire NG32 1HQ, UK.
Pots & Containers photograph pp 24-25 © Pots and Pithoi, The Barns, East Street,
    Turners Hill, West Sussex RH10 4QQ UK


Typeface: Veljovic & Geometric
Colour separation: Viscan Graphics (Singapore)
Printed in China by Sun Fung Offset Binding Co Ltd.

# CONTENTS

# Naming Plants

Plants are grouped, or classified, according to common characteristics. The names they are given indicate to which group they belong. The largest grouping, based on the structure of the plant's flowers, fruits and other organs, is the family. The family is then divided into genera and the genera into species. Every plant has a botanical name which is composed of two parts, the first indicating its genus and the second its species (written in italics). Species may be further divided into subspecies (subsp.).

Additional names indicate whether the subject is a hybrid (a cross between different genera or species, shown by ×), a cultivar (a man-made variation; the result of breeding, beginning with a capital letter in single quotes), a variety (a naturally occurring variation as opposed to a man-made one, var.) or a form (a plant with only a minor, but generally noticeable variation from the species, f.). Series or groups are collections of hybrid cultivars of like parentage.

Many plants are known by two names, or have been known by another name in the past; to avoid confusion, these names may be given as synonyms (syn.). Common names (colloquial, everyday names) are also used.

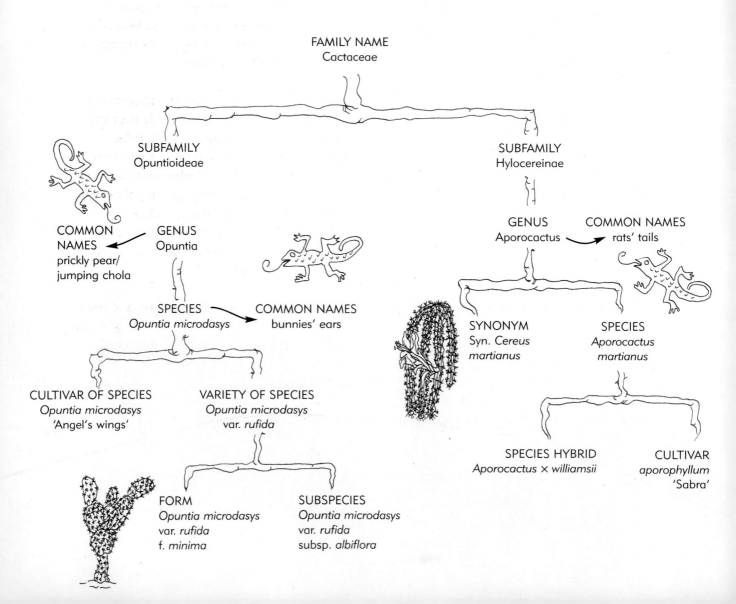

FAMILY NAME
Cactaceae

SUBFAMILY
Opuntioideae

SUBFAMILY
Hylocereinae

COMMON NAMES
prickly pear/
jumping chola

GENUS
Opuntia

GENUS
Aporocactus

COMMON NAMES
rats' tails

SPECIES
*Opuntia microdasys*

COMMON NAMES
bunnies' ears

SYNONYM
Syn. *Cereus martianus*

SPECIES
*Aporocactus martianus*

CULTIVAR OF SPECIES
*Opuntia microdasys*
'Angel's wings'

VARIETY OF SPECIES
*Opuntia microdasys*
var. *rufida*

SPECIES HYBRID
*Aporocactus* × *williamsii*

CULTIVAR
*aporophyllum*
'Sabra'

FORM
*Opuntia microdasys*
var. *rufida*
f. *minima*

SUBSPECIES
*Opuntia microdasys*
var. *rufida*
subsp. *albiflora*

# Foreword

My lifetime's interest in the world of cacti and other succulents began in the late 1950s. During this period literature on the subject was extremely limited and, when discovered, was mostly written not for the beginner but for the dedicated grower who could be expected to own a greenhouse.

Over the intervening years, thankfully, the situation has changed markedly for the better. Much more literature is available, with genuinely constructive advice for anyone interested in growing these distinctive plants.

As this new book by Shirley-Anne Bell reveals, there are immense possibilities in the centrally-heated home of today for displaying cacti and other succulents successfully without that once obligatory greenhouse. Not only does she give us copious information on their successful cultivation both in the home and in the conservatory, but her hints on care and maintenance, together with her advice on the use of modern composts and pest controls, demonstrate that living with these beautiful and generally undemanding plants should be a delight rather than a chore.

The interest in cacti and succulent plants in general has increased considerably over the past few years, and it appears still to be expanding as people realize just how varied and adaptable they are. Shirley-Anne and her husband Neville have been growing them for the past thirty years or more, and her knowledge on the subject shines through a book which is as attractively presented as it is singularly well-timed.

I for one certainly wish that this type of book had been around back in the 50s. The general reader, I am sure, will find it inspirational.

*Tom Jenkins*
*Chairman*
*British Cactus and Succulent Society*

# Introduction
# THE INDOOR GARDEN

Keen gardeners who live in unpredictable climates will do everything in their power to lengthen the hours of enjoying their plants, and an attractive solution is to give them a warm and protected environment inside. In the house their colours will enliven windowsills, table tops and shelves, while in a conservatory or sun lounge they should spread and bloom outrageously.

The indoor gardener's dream is to sit among dense greenery in the slightest sun, extending the season by several weeks in an unheated structure and by several months in a heated one – and yet, alas, harsh reality all too often fails to justify that initial optimism. It is, indeed, perfectly possible to create a suitable environment inside, but ordinary house plants have a tendency to parch and shrivel in a centrally-heated home, while a conservatory made predominantly of glass can be leaf-scorchingly hot during the summer months and bone-numbingly cold in winter.

This scenario can be as grievous for gardeners as it is perilous for their plants. The necessary

High life: succulents can make dramatic displays, whether massed together or (as with this *Aporocactus flagelliformis*) given pride of place with a few well-chosen ornaments.

non-stop summer watering, for example, creates a humid haze of condensation reminiscent of a rain forest, damaging those fine cane chairs. Going away becomes difficult without arranging for a 'sitter', and even an unexpectedly late return home may result in catastrophically wilting leaves. Time and money has to be spent on ventilation and drainage, heaters, sun blinds and double-glazing. It is possible, in short, to spend a good deal more time looking after our plants than getting pleasure from them.

Before you hurl the catalogues away and abandon your idea of a personal green paradise, consider the succulent solution – which is to enjoy a flexible space with the minimum of time, trouble and expense. Cacti and other succulents are not only striking and colourful, but they suit a hectic lifestyle, tolerating far more neglect than the more commonly grown indoor plants.

Something for everyone: from gigantic to miniscule, from prickly to hairy and fleshy, this family contains an amazing variety of distinctive plants.

## INFINITE VARIETY

There are succulents for every part of the conservatory and the home. Many of them grow naturally in relatively inhospitable habitats and will relish a certain amount of shade: these include the **epiphytic** cacti, such as epiphyllums, the glorious flowering orchid cacti, which have long strap-like stems; the flowering kalanchoes; and the hoyas with their glossy leaves and unusual waxy blooms.

Unfortunately, these easy-going plants are often badly served by being displayed in dusty corners of garden centres and shops. Although this demonstrates their powers of endurance (other plants would be dead), you rarely see them at their well-grown best. As a result, few people realize how variable and good-looking they can be. As well as the uncompromising columns and spheres of the traditional prickly cacti, the other succulents come in a diverse range of sizes, colours and shapes, from the sparse foliage of the angular or geometrical species, to the lush spreading habit of some of the bushier types.

Contrasts of shape and colour: this lush display
combines low-growing spreaders, a central
'statement' and cascading trailing plants in baskets.

Some will climb, trail and scramble. Some
are good for flowers, and although you may
picture cacti as nothing more than spiny
monsters covered in overcoats of ferocious
prickles, many will also flower like
clockwork every year. They bear an
assortment of magnificent, brightly coloured
blooms, forming a dazzling carpet of flowers.

Many of the 'other succulents' (see p. 7)
also flower readily. Some, like the winter-
flowering crassulas, can brighten up the
dreariest of the colder months. Their leaves
also offer a wonderful colour palette of

pinks, blues, lilacs and yellows, as well as
every shade of green, while variegated
forms have green leaves striped or splashed
with other colours.

No matter how big or small the space you
want to fill – from the tiniest windowsill to a
deep bay window or a huge conservatory –
there are plants for you to choose from, since
they range in size from the tiniest miniatures
to triffid-like monsters. Your display may have
a backdrop of tall specimen plants, along with
a wide variety of those which hang, trail and
climb; a middle ground filled with lower-
growing subjects; and a foreground of tiny
gems or unusual curiosities. Because many of
these plants produce remarkably large
flowers, you can move containers around to
give a changing seasonal display of colour.

You will find that the plants make an unusual
and original display, and their architectural
forms make them particularly sympathetic
choices for contemporary homes and garden
rooms. If you don't want to go the whole hog,
however, there is also a strong case for a
mixed conservatory: use succulent plants for
trouble-free mass planting and you will have
time to look after more demanding displays,
such as hanging baskets and containers filled
with colourful annuals like petunias and busy
lizzies for summertime special effects.
Alternatively, you can choose a few special
plants, like miniature citrus, olives or some of
the lovely subtropical plants such as
strelitzias, monstera and dracaena.

## CONVENIENCE

Succulent plants are relatively cheap to look
after. Many will thrive in an unheated space
or in an area that is kept just free from frost,

rather than needing the high temperatures of the sub-tropical species. Many, too, are also very easy to reproduce from offsets and cuttings, enabling you to turn a single plant into a satisfying massed display.

Most of the arguments for choosing cacti and other succulents to achieve a stylish, well-filled and, above all, easy-to-care-for conservatory can also be applied to using cacti as houseplants. Although there is a space for them in any window, they are an expecially good choice for south-facing sills and other impossibly sunny positions that will not support the average houseplant. Larger specimens will make a tolerant and unusual display in hot porches and entrance halls which are flooded with light, and they won't suffer in those long hours when you are not at home and the house has to be shut up tight against both intruders and ventilation.

All plants, of course, require light and water for healthy growth. Providing sufficient light and moisture in the relatively dim and dry atmosphere of an interior room can be difficult, and when you are displaying normal houseplants you often need to stand them in trays of pebbles and water in order to surround them with a moist microclimate. Misting is another essential for thirstier specimens, and this can prove troublesome if you have polished surfaces, tablecloths, pictures or susceptible wall coverings.

Cacti and succulents, on the other hand, need much less moisture than other plants. Just as in conservatories, this makes them tolerant companions, happy to withstand periods of neglect without lasting harm. It's true that they need relatively high light levels, but this in turn allows them to be used in positions which would literally be the death of most other plants. In the colder months, when many foliage house plants are far from at their best, you will find that your cacti and other succulents make a long-lasting, attractive and relatively unchanging display.

Lazy days: these plants will thrive on benign neglect.

They are also more resistant to such common nuisances as greenfly and red spider mite, while any pests they do have are relatively easy to treat. The only real scourge is the dreaded mealy bug (see p. 52), and luckily this is both slow-moving and susceptible to various insecticidal treatments, as well as being a candidate for biological control. Fungal infection can be a problem, because these plants lack the resistance to moulds and fungi that our native species have developed through originating in a damp climate. As this is yet another reason not to spend time on watering, however, this problem can be seen as a blessing in disguise.

As they like it: cacti and other succulents enjoy sunny positions which would scorch many other plants.

## ABOUT THIS BOOK

Although cacti and the other succulents have traditionally been displayed in a collection, often in nothing more inviting than formal rows of neatly labelled pots, these drought-resistant plants have such fantastic potential for the creation of exciting displays that they have plenty to offer the non-collector, too.

Acquiring and managing the traditional collection is a fascinating hobby which can lead to anything from competing on the show bench to visiting plant habitats in the Arizona desert or the South African Cape. To some avid collectors there is nothing more interesting than shampooing the shaggy white locks of a potentially prize-winning old man cactus (oreocereus) ready for the next show appearance. Other enthusiasts will study field collection numbers or ache to acquire the final available member of the escobaria genus. Even to the less passionate these plants offer a combination of beauty and convenience, not to speak of time saved for other activities.

This book is written not for the committed cactophile (although you may, of course, turn into one), but for anyone who wants to enjoy these wonderful plants without wishing to devote inordinate amounts of time to looking after them and finding out about them. It offers a quick route to learning which species to consider, how to look after them and how to propagate them, and it is designed so that you can find exactly what you need to know in easy-to-navigate sections.

The opening chapters cover organizing a display; devising planting schemes from containers through to permanent beds; and maintaining and propagating your plants. They will help you place and care for your plants in a range of settings. Inside the house itself you may wish to consider anything from a collection of tiny miniatures to a single large architectural plant. A sun lounge or conservatory may be a living space you can accessorize with a few really striking plants, or more of a plant room which you choose to fill with massed foliage in a large-scale display.

The second part of the book is a plant selector, with easy-to-follow lists designed for various types of display both in the home and in the conservatory – from miniature gems to large accent planting, and from trailing and flowering choices to assorted curiosities large and small. The best species to use are described in each chapter, and pictured both in inspirational settings and in close-ups which clearly reveal their characteristics.

Plant terms are printed in bold and explained in the glossary at the back of the book, where you will also find an appendix giving suggestions for further reading, together with details of cactus societies, websites and other sources of information.

## WHAT SUCCULENTS ARE

This book emphasizes use and display rather than botanical detail, but a digression is necessary to explain the features which make these plants a homogeneous group.

First, all **cacti** are **succulents**, but not all succulents are cacti. For convenience, therefore, I will generally refer to cacti and 'other succulents'.

Succulence in plants is usually an adaptation to periods of prolonged drought and conditions of extreme heat. Plants in this situation need to slow down **transpiration**, through which water is lost from their tissues. As a result many succulents have a reduced surface area to avoid water loss, as well as highly developed adaptations for storing what little moisture there is.

Great and small: compact specimens are ideal for miniaturist table-top displays, contrasting vividly with spreading plants such as the magnificent *Agave americana* 'Variegata' (left) with its variegated leaves.

Water can be stored in leaves, stems or roots. In stem succulents the stems are green because they have, to a greater or smaller extent, taken over the function of leaves and contain **chlorophyll**. Cacti are the best known of the stem succulent plants. They have adapted in the most extreme way, in that their shape has become simplified, with the stem becoming a water-storing sphere or column, with a covering of thick wool or spines evolved from leaves, for protection from the heat and from grazing animals. The **spines** grow from the distinctive **areoles**. They often have **ribs** and **tubercles**, although some are smooth: their shapes are geometrical, forming columns and spheres. (See below.)

The so-called 'other succulents', i.e. anything which is succulent other than cacti, have a variety of protective stratagems to deal with the stresses of drought and excessive heat. The stem succulents amongst them are distinguishable because they have fleshy ribbed or jointed stems, often with tubercles, and any leaves are **vestigial** if they are present at all. Among some of the leaf succulents,

such as lithops and other living stones, the leaves have become simplified into a fissured pair of pebble-like structures. In other cases they have developed tight, interlocking and overlapping structures, forming columns or rosettes; or their leaves have become thickened with a glossy, water-retentive surface; or they have developed a soft, reflective, light-coloured down.

The members of the final group are known as the **caudiciforms**. These are the real curiosities among what is already a very distinctive group of plant species. They have a hugely swollen **caudex** at the base of the plant, which is either an engorged root, an engorged section of stem or a combination of the two. These plants often produce twining flowering stems.

The advantage of this adaptation to their surroundings is that most of the cacti and other succulents are easy to care for. Not only

STRUCTURE OF CACTUS

Flower and bud arising from areole

Radial spines

Areole surrounding spines

Central spine

Tubercle

Ribs

are they **drought-resistant**, but they will also tolerate strong sunlight. This gives great flexibility, in that you can water and feed your plants when you choose to, rather than when you have to. They can be left when you go away, and you can relax after a busy day instead of needing to work on your plants: you can enjoy them instead of worrying about them.

## A NOTE ABOUT NAMES

Cacti and the other succulents have fewer common names than many other house and garden plants. Although you will therefore have to get to grips with a certain amount of Latin, the universal language of botany, this means that you can be certain that you are talking about the same plant whatever your background, country or mother tongue.

Needless to say, there is always a downside to the best of schemes. One, pronunciation, is easily disposed of. When I was at school we were taught that ancient Romans spoke, surprisingly, rather like Eton schoolboys, whereas my daughter was advised to use a sing-song accent like modern-day Italians. The answer is simply to take your pick – and say it with confidence!

The other point is more serious. In the botanical world, cacti and other succulents have suffered under the successive naming regimes of 'clumpers' and 'splitters'. This means that **genera** have been absorbed into one another on the one hand, or divided and subdivided on the other. As a result, the **botanical nomenclature** is complicated, and I would ask you to bear this in mind when reading this book. On the whole, I have taken a middle road, keeping the genera in what I

Moody: the strange shapes of many cacti and other succulents lend themselves to the creation of special effects.

hope are their best known and most easily recognized identities, and where it is helpful to the plant buyer I have retained the older form. As an example, chamaecereus or peanut cacti are very distinctive in appearance (sufficiently so to have a common name) and they include a wide range of named **cultivars**, so I have kept the **genus** name although strictly speaking they are now listed under lobivia. By the same token, in order to save confusion I have kept echinopsis and trichocereus separate, because one is so distinctive as a small, readily flowering genus, while the other is useful for larger, accent types of planting.

Appearance tends to be the final arbiter. For a conservatory or indoor display rather than an academic collection you will be selecting your plants according to whether you like their looks in terms of shape, spines, flowers or whatever. To this end, therefore, the book is fully illustrated with at least one example of nearly every genus mentioned, and often with many different **species**, and this should help you decide what will look best in your particular setting.

# Chapter 1
# Displaying Your Plants

Whether you have a small windowsill or a large conservatory, a skilful arrangement of your plants will help show off their special features to best advantage

Inside and out: a design which begins inside and flows out into the garden.

Throughout this book I emphasize the fantastic display potential that you have in cacti and other succulents. Try to arrange your indoor plants with the same considerations of colour, height and so on as you would employ when planning a garden. Outside, for instance, bulbs look best in clumps, with colours and species drifting in and out of one another, rather than being planted in stiff rows so that they march around in single line like soldiers on parade. Indoors your room for manoeuvre may be much more limited, but the same basic aesthetic rules apply.

You do need, however, to consider the conditions in which you are planning to show off these wonderful drought-resistant choices. Although this chapter is divided between conservatory and indoor display, there is obviously a continuum between the two different kinds of space.

Three dimensional: an embellishment of the above, with a view from a planted windowsill down to the conservatory and beyond.

Sometimes a modern, luxury conservatory may become an extension of the home, and will be used for dining, sitting or relaxing. Apart from enjoying more light, it will – in terms of double-glazing, blinds, curtains, carpets and so on – have all the features of a typical indoor room. In this case you will need to use plant saucers, trays and stands to protect your expensive furnishings from water or compost staining. Because the room has a specific function, such as dining, you will also probably want the plants to accessorize rather than to dominate the space, and some of the indoor plantings and displays may have more appeal to you.

In other cases your conservatory may be much more of an external room. Lean-to structures added to outside walls can be halfway houses between indoors and outdoors. They will often have no blinds or curtains, and they may be equipped with more durable, patio-style furnishing and brushable concrete floors to withstand water spillage. In these structures it is possible to

The hard stuff: the range of materials suitable for a conservatory includes (left to right) gravel, black and white chippings, slate, white chippings/dolomite, pea shingle, larger gravel pieces and white cobbles.

introduce a much more plant-orientated display, with raised areas, further beds in the ground and massed displays that can be watered with less fear of damage.

This continuum has the potential of allowing your planting to flow from your home, through the conservatory and out into the garden. Some of my photographs (see facing page) show a windowsill planting overlooking a conservatory in which an indoor rockery meets full-length windows and appears to merge into a hardy garden rockery: the three areas are linked together with a great feeling of continuity and of extra space. There are also practical considerations. Houseplants can have something of a holiday in the brighter-lit conservatory, while **half-hardy** plants can move outside in the summer to enjoy the daylight and fresh air. You also have the scope for exotic gardening to flow through into permanent garden planting schemes as described in my companion book *Growing Cacti and Other Succulents In the Garden*.

## CONSERVATORIES

Most plant-orientated conservatories which are used as plant rooms rather than as home extensions look at their best if they are generously planted. Think of your display as a painting, with a foreground, middle ground and background. Ideally you are hoping to strike a balance by using a variety of plants, with differences in height, shape, colour and size. And do allow some informality and

happy, unforeseen juxtapositions: a rigid and over-formal display, such as a line of pots with no variation, is usually off-putting.

In the conservatory, therefore, think of grouping your plants together like a mini border. As well as choosing taller plants, climbers and hanging subjects to give your displays height, the ideal format uses an array of staging, with some higher level benching at the top and plants arranged in a number of levels descending from this point, like a staircase. Ideally, you need several tall-growing '**accent**' plants, which will give a strong vertical line, interspersed with squatter, lower-growing plants, plus species which will cascade down and soften the formal geometrical lines of the benches.

For displaying your plants, one of the most elegant solutions is to use Chelsea plant stands, also known as *étagères des fleurs*, which are ready-constructed series of shelves designed to fit along walls. You can also buy corner stands to continue the display right round the walls. For 'elegant', however, you can also read 'expensive'.

Step by step: a display stand is ideal if you have space for it.

You can also construct your own stepped **staging**, which is a much cheaper option if you or another family member is keen on DIY. Another alternative, quick and cheap, is to use Toplite blocks or similar lightweight construction blocks. Give them a good coat of white paint to seal the surface, as the undecorated surfaces are rather crumbly. They make instant lightweight shelving, which can be moved or changed as often as you like. They also look very good, rather like 1930s international-style modernist architecture: think of brilliant white cubist houses by Le Corbusier with severe horizontals and verticals. You can arrange them in a series of stepped arrangements, using different faces, and they are so cheap that you can change them if they begin to show unsightly stains.

As the Toplite is soft, you can easily hollow out shapes in it, using a wood drill or a chisel, and then either plant directly into it or insert your plants while they are still in their pots. Breeze blocks are another cheap support, with rot-proof timber shelving placed across them. You can build more than one level, and the whole thing can be taken apart and altered whenever you please.

The illustrations show an abstract, geometrical conservatory display with two alternative planting schemes. The first uses succulents as miniature bonsai trees, planted in a series of shallow dishes and top-dressed with a variety of materials, such as tumble-polished pebbles, slate and flint. Chinese dragon dogs add to the eastern feel. The second scheme has echeverias and other plants with almost flower-like rosettes displayed individually in stark, shiny black geometrical dishes, with large candles and cobbles to give a good *feng shui*.

These kinds of display also lend themselves to interesting and good-looking interior schemes. A room divider, a series of stepped shelves or one of those flexible furniture cupboard and shelving cube systems, such as the Cubestore range, would all look just as good accesorized with the same kind of plant displays as the ones used in the conservatory scheme shown here.

Trellis and other supports can look very attractive, and you have the option of allowing plants to clamber up from base level or of attaching containers to the trellis in any position from the top downwards for attractive trailing. Trellis comes in a variety of shapes, with plain or swagged tops, and you can either retain the natural colour or choose from the fantastic palette of wood stains and finishes now on the market. Trellis and screens are also available with shiny metal finishes, and there are some new coloured plastic versions which may sound nasty but are actually very good-looking and will last almost indefinitely.

Keeping it simple: these miniature displays have an oriental feel, the two on the left featuring bonsai succulents. Designs like this are said to give good *feng shui*.

Space-filler: Toplite is an infinitely adaptable staging material, and can be assembled to fill any area you choose.

The widely available freestanding obelisks, made from wrought iron or woven cane and withies, can be used inside as well as outside in the garden. There are all sorts of wire frames, too. Look at topiary shapes, such as cones, hoops and balls, or even comedy livestock (birds, dogs and so on), which can be completely covered with unusual clambering succulents. Alternatively, choose spiral plant supports for a display of climbing plants in a long trough or in a camouflaged grow bag. There are also futuristic forms in shiny aluminium which can look very chic in a modern interior.

Hanging pots and baskets, wall-mounted containers filled with **trailing** other succulents or some of the unusual hanging cacti such as aporocacti, or rats' tails, make wonderful space-filling conversation pieces. They are so easy to look after that you can have masses of them without worrying about keeping them watered daily, as you must with traditional water-guzzling baskets. You can also have an abundance of pots fastened to walls, where succulent plants will spread so happily that this is where the drought resistance of these plants can be fully appreciated. As well as traditional baskets, there are decorative metal or cane bird cages which are far kinder to plants than they are to anything with feathers, plus futuristic spiral designer baskets in galvanized steel. Look, too, for openwork free-standing urns, which are meant for lining with moss and planting through the sides.

You can add all kinds of interesting containers that can be moved around to vary the planting. They might, for instance, be taken out of the house to enhance your plant displays in the garden before returning to the conservatory – for a period of recuperation, if necessary, or just to ring the changes. You also have the option of creating internal beds, raised up or at ground level, into which you can plant massed displays.

Hang 'em high: *Aporocactus flagelliformis* is ideal for hanging pots and baskets.

Sun bathers: a windowsill comes to life with a colourful array of succulents.

## IN THE HOME

Many homes have south-facing windows which are hostile to ordinary plants, but which can look very barren without any pots on display. Even in the most uncompromising positions, however, cacti and sun-loving succulents such as the living stones will flourish happily, delighting you with regular displays of flower each year.

A normal windowsill will hold a range of small plants in pots and interesting containers, or can feature a row of spiny monsters. You can also add a second level of trailing plants, attached to hooks screwed into the top of the window recess.

A deep windowsill gives an increased scope for massed planting. It enables you to use accent plants, trailing or hanging subjects and a wide range of heights and shapes of cacti and other succulents. Using a table or shelf unit against the window can also provide additional display space in a sunny spot. Keep cacti and the living stones nearer

to the glass and arrange other succulents, which will tolerate a little more shade, further into the room.

Chapters 6 to 10 in this book are arranged to make choosing your plants easy. Windowsills lend themselves especially well to flowering plants, described in Chapter 9, and some of the lower-growing curiosities in Chapter 10, which features the likes of **living stones**, caudiciforms, **bonsai**-like succulents and characterful cacti such as old man of the mountains.

These smaller displays are also extremely useful for the elderly and infirm who can no longer enjoy the pleasure of large-scale outdoor gardening. A plant collection can be assembled on a trolley which can be rolled in and out of position inside a sunny window.

Care of a windowsill collection is really simple. In the growing season, water your plants roughly once a week, ensuring that they dry out completely first. As always, if in doubt, don't water. A few extra days without it when you are away will not be a problem to your plants, although you should give them a good drink when you get back. Feed them every four or six weeks in the growing season – and do pot them on each spring if they appear to be cramped.

Because your light source is necessarily one-sided, rotate the plants every two weeks or so to ensure that they grow evenly and don't become lopsided.

## OTHER BRIGHTLY LIT SPACES

In houses, there are often other awkward spaces that cannot sustain ordinary houseplants. Bright, hot entrance halls with light pouring in through glassed doors can create impossible environments for foliage plants. Houses of the sixties and seventies vintage with large picture windows can also be difficult, while new homes in converted lofts and studios also often have large windows, which can be hostile to many plants.

Here you can introduce the sort of massed planting described and illustrated for conservatories, but on a smaller scale. Large, high-impact groups of cacti and succulents in attractive containers can look fabulous displayed next to pieces of sculpture. A really well-lit space can also be used for some lavish hanging displays, like aporocactus and kalanchoe, which produce colourful arrays of flower in the spring and early summer as well as unusual or lush foliage displays.

In an unheated greenhouse or conservatory water is reduced in the autumn. Over the winter the plants are allowed to become totally dry and dormant, and they will then withstand temperatures down to freezing.

However, in a house just as in a heated conservatory, the higher temperatures mean that your plants will not become completely dormant in the winter. They will, as a result, require occasional watering – and this, in turn, will make them more susceptible to the cold. Since windowsills can become very inhospitable places in winter, take care not to draw the curtains over your plants or they will suffer in that chilly space between the window and the room. The safest precaution in the coldest weather is to pull down a blind or tuck the curtains behind your plants.

Top to bottom: a waterfall of succulent foliage fills this picture window, with little maintenance required to keep it in prime condition.

## SUNNY PORCHES

Sunny porches can also be a problem for attractive plant displays. They obviously have to be kept closed up for security reasons when you are out at work, shopping or visiting, so temperatures can be blisteringly high and conditions very dry.

Again, these are another ideal site for cacti and succulent displays. At the nursery we have often 'adopted' refugees from porches, which have grown to such astonishing proportions that their owners can no longer accommodate them. This, therefore, is an ideal spot for some larger growing specimens, as described in Chapter 6, with either jumbo specimens, or a small group of tall plants, making a great impact. Don't forget the upper spaces, which can also be filled with a cascade of tolerant hanging choices.

Like unheated conservatories, porches benefit from **borrowed heat** from the house: you have a frost-free space ideal for a wide range of plants. In this case, it is best to gradually withdraw water altogether from the autumn onwards until the plants are bone dry over the winter months. You can gradually resume watering from the early spring onwards.

Porches can also act as another useful asylum space for large, half-hardy containers that spend the summer months out of doors but need winter protection. Larger subjects like agaves and massed containers of echeverias or other succulents can often be fitted into a porch when the house just could not accommodate them.

## COMMERCIAL PREMISES

Cacti and succulents also lend themselves to display in office and business premises, where their low maintenance and their tolerance of hot and dry conditions is a great benefit, because they can cope with periods of neglect that would kill most other plants. The sunny windows in large office blocks or the light atriums and reception areas can be vastly improved with these robust and good-looking plants, rather than some of the dusty and wilting specimens that find their place there, or, worse still, the artificial specimens which are sometimes used.

Sunny frontages, such as car showrooms and offices that are open-fronted to attract clients, can take large-scale planting in raised beds, and this will promote more rapid growth.

Set in stone: a rockery suits the wide open spaces of a showroom or an office reception area.

## CACTI AND SUCCULENTS AS INTERIOR DECOR

There is a growing trend towards using a single really dramatic larger plant as a design feature in its own right, just as you might use a piece of sculpture or an art work. Because cacti and succulents have such dramatic and architectural shapes, you may have noticed that adverts and magazine articles are increasingly featuring them, either as individual plants or as dramatic groupings, in strong, accent plantings.

Cacti and succulents are much favoured in modern, more minimalist interiors, because if you have spent time and money creating a cutting edge formal décor without fussy details, then these sculptural plants make an ideal addition. They fit well with bold colours and simple shapes, as well as with stark black and white, or chrome and glass.

Specimen plants are not cheap, especially when chosen from among the true cacti, because a large plant represents many years of growth. A large specimen, on the other hand, will make a very strong feature on its own, so the costs can balance out.

However, if you compare the cost of a piece of sculpture or even a really nice lamp, then tall opuntias arranged as a matching pair on either side of a fireplace will make a showy and dramatic talking point which is well worth the expense.

A large plant can transform that 'Cinderella' corner of a room. A single cactus such as a cereus or cleistocactus, or a quick-growing branched succulent look-alike chosen from the euphorbias, would make a striking feature plant for an alcove or a niche. It could also stand on a wall table or plinth. The taller-growing plants described in Chapter 6 give you numerous species to choose from. In a single display like this, it's worth giving the plant a really attractive container and incorporating other features – glass beads, perhaps, candles and ornaments, or polished stones spilling from clear jars.

Foreign accent: *Aeonium arboreum* 'Zwartkop' from the Canary Islands is a popular choice of feature plant with interior designers. In front is an *Agave americana* 'Variegata'.

Highly regarded: a pedestal raises this pot of *Crassula ovata* 'Hummel's Sunset' to a height at which it can be justifiably admired.

Try, for example, combining the silvery spines of white-haired cacti with a stark black and silver scheme of wall covering, table covers and ornaments. Bright ethnic pots in reds and yellows look good with opuntias and branching euphorbias. Tiny dishes of pebbles associate well with the living stones, and terracotta pots and ornaments relate sympathetically, too. You might, on the other hand, prefer to go for an oriental feel with massive church candles, a fat Buddha and a bonsai-like arrangement of succulents or knobbly caudiciforms.

A set of shelves, perhaps acting as a room divider and therefore as a decorative rather than purely functional unit, can take a row of large fat mammillarias or unusual **cristate** forms which can be viewed from every angle.

A stark wall can be enhanced with a huge, contorted specimen like a caudiciform plant or a cristate cereus. Alternatively a tall, **candelabrum**-shaped euphorbia, the pale columns of *Cleistocactus strausii* or a 1m x 1m (3ft x 3ft) *Crassula ovata* makes a fabulous small indoor tree.

Obviously, when you are using plants as design features, you will not necessarily be able to give them the brightly lit spots in which they will flourish for long periods. You will often want the plants to fit in with you rather than allowing them to dictate the position they would prefer to occupy: you may, for example, want to display them in less than favourable positions for their sculptural and architectural qualities.

Cacti and succulents will tolerate short periods in dull conditions, but they cannot be left for long without suffering. Like all plants, they need light for the production of the chlorophyll which allows them to manufacture food in order to grow, flower and possibly set seed. Without good light, cacti and other succulents become **etiolated**, with pale and spindly new growth which looks ugly and is obviously detrimental to their health.

One option is to use a variety of plants for short periods, moving them in and out of position, and taking them out of less hospitable areas before there is any damage. Give them a good rest back in a well-lit position and they will be fit to make regular reappearances. You can use any brightly lit space as a recovery unit, from a south-facing windowsill to a sunny porch, a picture window or a conservatory. The ideal in this case is to have a 'cast' of plants that can make a starring appearance and then have a period of resting – like most actors!

You can, however, also combine these strong plants with artificial lighting to create a really spectacular permanent feature in a room. This is obviously a better solution when you are dealing with expensive plants and you are understandably determined to get your money's worth from your investment.

Plants need both red and blue light for growth and photosynthesis. Red light (6,000 to 7,000 angstroms) is especially important to flowering plants, because it is necessary for the production of flower and seed. With this alone, though, the plants make spindly, elongated growth, so you also need blue light (4,000 to 5,000 angstroms) for leaf development. You must have both, as blue light on its own also creates problems, with thickening stems, short growth, darkening of the leaves and poor flower growth

In part of your room that receives a reasonable amount of light, you can combine natural light with artificial lighting as a supplement. In this case, any lamp which can be switched on for two or three hours in the morning and again in the evening will be appropriate. The plants will continue to make healthy and compact growth, while the lighting feature itself will enhance the appearance of the plant.

In a poorly lit area, such as a hearth or room corner, you could nevertheless position a table or a plant stand to grow exciting feature plants which can remain there for long periods without coming to any harm. However, the normal incandescent light bulbs used in table lamps, wall lights and overhead fitments are no longer appropriate here, because it would be necessary to use them for long periods and these incandescent bulbs unfortunately emit both red light and infrared radiation. Over long periods they produce a lot of heat, which will damage the plants, and they also concentrate the light, so that it will only cover a restricted area.

In this case, fluorescent lighting is a far better option, because the tubes stay much cooler and the light covers a wider area. Fluorescent lights give out over twice as much light per watt as normal incandescent equivalents, and they also have differing combinations of red and blue light. Houseplants, including cacti and other succulents, demand a combination of cool white and warm white for optimum growth. Note that you can also buy special lights which are designed to optimize plant growth, such as Gro-Lux or Plant-Gro.

Bright idea: cacti and other succulents can look dramatic under artificial lighting, but the kind of light you give them is important.

Fluorescent tubes come in a range of fittings, so don't worry that you must have utilitarian strip lights which look as if they belong in the office or kitchen. Strip lights are often appropriate, of course – for example, when they can be fitted neatly under shelving in order to down-light plant arrangements. You

Highs and lows: this artificially lit display has been carefully arranged to provide interest from a variety of viewpoints, with the largest plants standing at the back.

can also use unobtrusive circular fitments with a variety of shades. Shades or hoods have the advantage of directing the light, which has the benefit of giving the plants a dramatic presence in your room – rather as you would use spotlights to display pictures on walls, or ornaments or statues in arches and on plinths. Each square metre of growing space needs about 175 to 225 watts of light, with the lights positioned 30–45cm (12–18in) above the plants. Because the intensity of the tubes diminishes with time, you should aim to replace them annually.

Although you can grow your plants under fluorescent lights alone, probably the most pleasing arrangement is to combine both incandescent and fluorescent light. This may sound unnecessarily complicated, but it enables you to use really attractive light fitments as part of the plant feature you are creating: use two or three watts of fluorescent light to one watt of incandescent light to provide the right balance of light without overheating your arrangement.

You can also incorporate reflection into your arrangements. A mirror, pale wall surfaces, a silver table covering or chrome table tops will all reflect light onto the plants. This again offers the benefits of a really striking arrangement which both looks good and promotes plant growth.

In a commercial environment you may be looking for a very large and dramatic **architectural** planting, like a mini indoor desert. These corporate schemes obviously need lighting on a much larger scale. Commercial growers' systems are essential here, using high intensity discharge (HID) lights in which electricity flows through high-pressurized vaporized gas. There is a choice

of high-pressure sodium or metal halide lamps, but the metal halide lamps are the best solution of all, because they are the nearest you can get to natural daylight.

Looking In: the display on the opposite page is equally attractive when seen from outside.

# CHAPTER 2
# INTERESTING POTS AND CONTAINERS

The range available from garden centres and multiple DIY chains is huge, from low-cost terracotta, through wonderful coloured glazes to nesting families of painted pots

Up in the air: the translucence of the large planter allows the eye to focus on this magnificent trailing *Sedum sieboldii*.

natural light, while their leaves and stems seem to become stouter and more resilient as a result of their exposure to the elements. They make fine accent plantings for outside front doors, on steps, on patios and along paths. In the autumn they can move back inside, where they will continue to give you pleasure throughout the colder months. They can give you large and dramatic feature plants for the conservatory or porch, or make fabulously showy and unusual houseplants. If you are interested in this, see the companion volume *Growing Cacti and other Succulents in the Garden*.

Indoors and in the conservatory your containers have no need to be frost-resistant, which happily means that you have fewer constraints on choice. You will need to stand the pots in waterproof trays or saucers in order to protect windowsills, table-tops and other surfaces, but you also have the option of using **cachepots** – attractive outer pots without drainage holes into which you can slip the more functional plastic pots, concealing them in attractive 'sleeves'. You can use all sorts of other interesting bits and pieces, including 'found' containers such as cups and saucers, teapots and old casseroles.

Garden centres stock a huge range of containers which, thanks to economies of scale, are of surprisingly good value, but junk shops and car boot sales are a good source of interesting oddities that go well with these plants – a small flowering cactus in a porcelain cup and saucer, for instance, or a trailing plant issuing from the neck of an olive jar. Ideally you should provide drainage

There is endless scope for using cacti and succulents in attractive pots and containers in the house and in the conservatory. Displays are long-lasting and colourful, and they offer the advantage of portability so that you can ring the changes. When the pot looks at its best, perhaps with a mass of flowers, you can feature it prominently before moving it into a less conspicuous position when its hour of glory is over.

Using containers also allows you to move your planting into the garden while there is no danger of frost. Cacti and other succulents make wonderful half-hardy summer bedding plants, and they colour up intensely in holes in all of your containers because they can so easily and unexpectedly become waterlogged. If this is not possible, if you don't want to risk a fragile piece of china or if you are scared of damaging surfaces, then use a very gritty compost mix, and either mist the container occasionally or leave it rather longer than usual between waterings than you would otherwise do.

Household casualties can also be rehabilitated. Often there is a favourite cup or bowl that is too chipped to be of much use for its original purpose but has some sentimental value or is particularly pretty or funny, and you can press this into new and decorative service as a plant container.

Drainage holes can be added quite easily with an electric drill, but do wear goggles when you are doing this. You'll find that most containers can be drilled quite easily with a masonry drill on a slow speed: a cushion of foam or plasticine beneath the object you are drilling can help prevent fracture, as it will dampen the sudden shock of the drill breaking through.

Home sweet home: the unusual jar in the corner has found its proper role as a container for *Sedum morganianum* (donkeys' tails).

Mug's game: an old favourite now cracked but put to good use as a container for *Lithops lesliei*.

Baskets can also look very pretty. Staple a good lining of black polythene to the inside, or, if the weave isn't too open, apply two or three good coats of varnish or paint (enamel or gloss), and this will also do the trick. Again, don't forget to pierce some drainage holes through the polythene lining.

Strawberry pots are quite difficult to maintain when they are used for their intended purpose or to grow herbs, because they can be hard to keep sufficiently wet. They make good succulent containers, however, because these plants are so much more tolerant of drought. They look really attractive planted up with trailing succulents (see next page) or, for a complete change, with upright opuntias, so that there is an aspirational onwards-and-upwards feel to the pot instead.

New pots for old: a strawberry pot adapted for trailing succulents.

However, even when you do use succulent plants, it can be hard to give the compost a really good soaking, especially when you first plant the pot up. The narrow neck can result in water running down the outside rather than the inside of the pot. Solve this problem by inserting a length of sink pipe, cut to length and drilled with a series of regular perforations down the centre of the container. The top of the pipe should be higher than the surface of the compost to stop anything clogging up the pipe, although you can hide it with gravel. The bottom should finish 5-7.5cm (2-3in) above the bottom of the pot. If you water down into this pipe, the water will percolate evenly through the container and into each of the side pockets. (See above.)

A cascade pot makes another attractive container, which can be planted up with trailing succulents. This is where pots of the same appearance but different dimensions are stacked one on top of the other, wired together and planted up with trailing succulents around the rim with a centrepiece plant in the topmost pot. For example, a stack of three round, glazed pottery containers in a rich cobalt blue can look stunning planted with grey-leaved or green-and-gold variegated succulent plants.

There are two methods of fastening the pots together – which is necessary, because there is a lot of weight, especially in pottery structures, and you don't want your work of art to become dislodged, or to topple over and break.

In the first method, measure a length of stiff wire, long enough to pass through each pot in turn with plenty to spare. Anchor the wire in by bending it into an 'L' shape at the bottom and push it up through the drainage hole of the first pot. Fill the pot with a mixture of drainage material and compost, position the next pot above it and push the wire up through the drainage hole of the second pot. Centre it on top of the first and add compost. Repeat until you reach the topmost pot, pull the wire tight and bend it to secure the pots together before adding compost to the final pot and planting up. (See left.)

Pots within pots: two types of self-made cascade pot, as described above.

Good companions:
pink-flowered *Crassula cooperi*, hairy-leaved *Echeveria setosa* and trailing *Crassula sarmentosa*, here grouped together in a bowl garden, demonstrate the effectiveness of contrasts.

The second method is much easier. Cut a length of bamboo cane, and position it above the central drainage hole of the first pot and anchor it in place with stones or pebbles. Fill with compost, and then centre the second pot over the first by lowering it over the cane. Carry on until you have your tower, with everything fastened together by this central rod. (See left.) After filling the final pot with compost, cut the excess cane away and plant up as desired.

As well as a variety of pots and containers, you can also get an interesting range of materials for top dressing them. Look at blue slate, which goes from pale grey when dry to glossy blue-black when wet. Dolomite is stark and white and goes well with white cobbles. Black and white chippings can look very dramatic, while the natural tones of mixed gravels and shingles give a lovely warm honey glow to pots.

Wherever you are planning to site your containers, consider a little 'set dressing'. A single pot can look a bit sorry for itself, so why not give it some suitable companions? The permutations are endless, but you might perhaps use interesting natural materials, such as shells and pebbles collected on holidays and outings: polished pebbles and marbles look fantastic spilling out of bowls and jars across a table top or shelf. You could also introduce other containers, such as pretty jugs, bottles and jars; ornaments and statues; and, in the house or a conservatory/house extension, lighting features such as candles, candlesticks and lamps, together with pictures, photographs and mirrors.

Textures: the scattering of small angular stones in this pot adds interest to the spiky display of *Pterocactus kuntzei*.

## CHOOSING PLANTS FOR CONTAINERS

Plant choices and descriptions are covered fully in their own respective chapters. For simplicity, I have divided the plants into large plants for accent planting; lower-growing choices; trailing and climbing plants grown for foliage colour and/or for their flowers; low-growing flowering plants; and feature plants such as the strange **living rocks** and bonsai-like succulent miniature trees.

Coordinates: the blue-green leaves of this *Scilla violacea* look splendid against the rich terracotta of its pot.

Trailing plants (see page 103) look well in both strawberry and cascade pots, where they can tumble out of the perforations or meander over the pot edges. You can try either a mixed planting or a single mass display of a novelty plant such as donkeys' tails (*Sedum morganianum*) or the string of beads (*Senecio rowleyanus*).

Any kind of container with a long stem and flat top, or a container placed strategically on an old cake stand, for example, also acts as a brilliant foil for hanging and cascading plants. Look out for flower arranging accessories: the shallow plastic bowls on a stem, meant to hold an oasis block, can be adapted to gush

pretty waterfalls of succulent leaves. The plants can be placed in a shallow container because they do not need a large root ball.

All of these plants make good hanging basket choices, without the nightmare chores of regular watering, feeding and deadheading. (I can't be the only one to have poured a full watering can first over my geraniums, then over my head and finally straight up the cuff of my sweater!) The flower-like rosettes of colourful echeverias studding the sides of a basket can also look very pretty. If you are planning to use hanging plants indoors, be sparing with watering and use a container with a built-in saucer to catch any drips. The safest method to protect your décor is to take the plant outside to water it.

Larger hanging plants can also be combined into very **low maintenance** hanging baskets. Flowering plants like epiphyllums (orchid cacti) and aporophyllums (rats' tails) make attractive drought-resistant basket choices with amazing flower displays, and these can be put into the background when flowering is over. Cloudy masses of foliage like rhipsalis are also effective, along with the more shade-tolerant kalanchoes and hoyas.

Long trail a-winding: another clever colour combination involving bronze terracotta pot, white dolomite and trailing *Sedum morganianum*.

Showing off: while the *Sedum nussbaumerianum* is encouraged to smother the edges of its large blue pot the *Dudleya antonyi* on the right is given a shallower container to display its distinctive trunk.

Tall accent plants like the aeoniums and agaves featured in Chapter 6 look well rising out of a carpet of scrambling and trailing succulents, which always have an attractive softening effect. And because the colour range of these plants is unusual, with pinks, purples, greys, maroon, bronze and turquoise – tones which are less frequently seen among the more conventional choice of plants – you have the scope to create some really unusual and exciting colour combinations.

Large bowls and other containers look fabulous filled with a mass planting of tiny, **globular**-flowering cacti such as rebutias, mammillarias and lobivias. They create a spectacular display in the spring and early summer, and are a novel alternative to the more commonly seen pots of spring-flowering bulbs.

Lithops or living stones are another unusual choice, especially when planted among a camouflage of rounded pebbles, from which (until they produce their white and yellow daisy heads of flower in the autumn) they can hardly be told apart. Children love these speckled choices. They often also enjoy the challenge of creating a miniature garden in a bowl, using the tiny succulent plants for

'grass', 'flowers' and 'trees', perhaps with a sliver of mirror and a balsa wood bridge leading to a pebble path. Cacti are perhaps too prickly for tiny fingers.

On the subject of succulent miniature trees in artificial landscapes, shallow containers, especially the large flat saucers designed to go with big glazed or terracotta bowls, make fabulous homes for any of the pretty succulents which can be used for instant bonsai as described in Chapter 10. Again, wearing eye protection you can easily drill drainage holes into the containers and finish the planting off with rocks and stones. Caudiciforms, with their bloated swollen roots like craggy rocks, also make interesting plants for saucers like these.

In the past, we have had a lot of fun with a pottery cat which lay indolently in a bowl of succulents while it 'fished' in a pond of blue and green *Echeveria derenbergii* and *E. subsesillis*. It looked very pretty and attracted a lot of interest and comment until it took up its proper function as a waterfall on the edge of an ornamental pond in the garden.

Bits and pieces: these contrasting succulents are planted among interesting stones and 'found' objects.

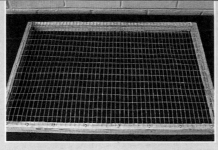

The materials: wooden frame; wire mesh; nails and staples; sphagnum moss.

Basic frame.

Echeveria plant with florists' wire.

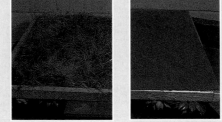

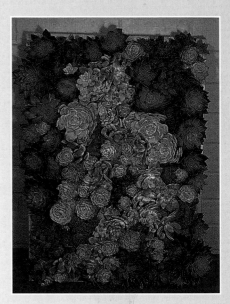

ABOVE LEFT: Upside down and supported on bricks.

ABOVE RIGHT: Back now fastened in place.

LEFT: Reverse showing wiring of plants.

INSET LEFT: The first echeveria attached.

RIGHT: The finished living picture.

Here's how to construct a fabulous living plant 'picture', complete with frame. First construct a shallow rectangular box of well-treated water-resistant wood, with a perforated base for drainage. Next line it with a good layer of sphagnum moss covered with wide-gauge wire mesh – making sure that there is space for the plant roots to be inserted through the gaps.

Design an abstract composition, or a really simple landscape such as sky, hill and lake, using contrasting colours of carpeting succulents – perhaps a mixture of sedums and crassulas, a selection of light and dark echeverias or a combination of plants which will retain a flat habit of growth. You can always experiment with coloured pencils on graph paper first, as you would if you were planning a knitting pattern or tapestry design.

A picture comprised solely of echeverias is instant, because you can wire them into place and move the box into a vertical position immediately. Usually the 'picture' will initially have to lie flat, although as the plants grow and the roots anchor the structure into place you will be able to tilt it by degrees until the whole thing is vertical. Water by misting thoroughly with a hand sprayer (or take it outside in hot weather and give it a good soaking with a watering can) and you will have an unusual centrepiece for your conservatory or garden room. Trim the sedums back with nail scissors, and pull out any extra plant material if it threatens to swamp your design. If you use echeverias with their flowers on long stalks do cut off any buds as they appear, or you may have a 'picture' more Dali-esque surreal than you care for.

Going to pot: containers need crocks to cover the drainage holes; compost mixed with horticultural grit; and gravel and rocks for surface decoration.

## CULTIVATION ADVICE FOR CONTAINERS

Cacti and succulents are unusual in that their main requirement is to dry out between waterings, and they dislike standing for long periods with 'wet feet' – especially when the weather is cool and dull. To protect them from overwatering, make sure that all your containers have a good layer of drainage material, which should be up to one third of a large pot. Those polystyrene chippings which are used as packing material have the advantage of being lightweight and free, although it has to be said that they are not very pleasant to use.

Compost requirements are quite flexible. You can use any houseplant compost, such as a multipurpose soilless compost, a peat-based compost or a John Innes soil-based compost (numbers 2 or 3 are fine), with the addition of horticultural grit for extra drainage to give you a safety margin if you are inclined to be heavy-handed with watering. A pedestal pot or a lightweight plastic pot is better with a soil-based compost, to prevent the container toppling when the compost is dry.

In the bleak midwinter: *Crassula 'Silver Springtime'* makes a pretty winter display of flowers, set off by its blue ceramic pot and white top dressing.

The plants are tolerant, but will appreciate a good soaking approximately once a week in the growing season and feeding roughly once a month. Between late autumn and early spring your plants should be kept dry and frost free. This dry period is essential for cacti if they are to set flower successfully the following year.

During the winter months, the 'other succulents' will need an occasional light misting in a warmer conservatory to keep them plump and hydrated, while the cacti will also need the bare minimum of water in order to prevent them from shrivelling.

You will find that many plants will survive in an unheated conservatory, but it then becomes of paramount importance to keep them as dry as possible, because the combination of wet and cold is lethal to these drought-resistant choices.

# Chapter 3
# LANDSCAPING YOUR CONSERVATORY

Raised beds, rockeries and water features are attractive possibilities
if you have the space for them

Luxury living: these opuntias and agaves are thriving in the space afforded by a large bed.

Although some conservatories are so much a part of the house that they have to be respected and furnished as another part of your internal living space, you may be fortunate enough to possess one which functions more as an interior garden and which can therefore accommodate a more radical treatment.

At its simplest this may take the form of incorporating raised planters, so that you can have a massed planting along the walls. Larger raised beds give a lot more scope to your imagination, but you may decide to go further and plant directly into the ground, creating your own interior desert or succulent forest.

You can elaborate this internal landscape even further by adding interior rockeries or water features which can either be freestanding, self-contained fountains or may take the form of a meandering mini stream and a tiny waterfall spilling into a small-scale pool – perhaps even complete with fish.

Other conservatories may function as multipurpose spaces where you may decide to keep birds, reptiles or even tropical butterflies. In this case, succulent planting gives a low-maintenance and attractive environment for both you and your wildlife to enjoy.

## PLANTING DIRECTLY INTO BEDS

Although it is not always an option, some conservatories do offer the possibility of planting directly into beds. You will find that your plants will flourish with a freer root run without being as likely to get out of hand as some of the more usual choices of conservatory plant, such as passion flower (passiflora). In their natural habitat, cacti in particular have developed wide-ranging but shallow root runs, and this can be simulated in a bed when it is just not possible in a normal-sized container.

Older style conservatories, added to the backs of houses, often have a thin concrete base which can be partially removed to make a border for planting up against the original house wall, just as you would do with an outside border. You also have the option of creating a raised bed but, since you must take care not to compromise the damp-proof course, the bed needs to be slightly forward of the house wall.

DAMP-PROOF
COURSE

Home and dry: in a conservatory with a thin concrete base you can plant directly into the ground below the damp-proof course, but a raised bed will need to be a freestanding, lined construction to avoid compromising the damp-proofing.

DAMP-PROOF
COURSE

Leg room: a raised bed gives plants more space for their roots and makes them easier to reach.

## RAISED BEDS

Raised beds do have certain advantages, in that they are easier for older or less able people to garden in, and they can also be designed to incorporate clever integral seating, which can look very attractive. The wide, flat tops of paving stones also offer flexible seating and a surface for drinks – a real bonus if you have parties in there. Raised beds also give an instant height and impact to your plant display, and can solve the problem of creating different levels.

At its simplest, a freestanding raised bed can be constructed from log roll, which comes in heights of either 15cm (6in) or 30cm (12in), depending on whether you want a deep bed or more of a kerb for lower growing species. Log rolls are useful in that you can wire them into any shape you wish, including swirling asymmetrical shapes or regular circles and ovals. If you want planting on a grand scale, you can make a series of curved beds with a path to meander through them – your own mini botanical garden – or you can make a double-decker bed by constructing a second one on top of the first to give some height to your planting displays. They can also be removed and changed more easily than any other kind of bed.

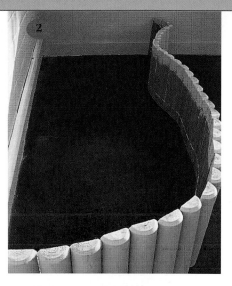

MAKING A RAISED BED FROM LOG ROLL:
1 & 2 Fix the roll securely to a wall.     3 Line with heavy-duty polythene.
4 Put in a layer of hard core topped with gravel.
To complete the job prior to planting, fill the bed with a free-draining mixture of compost and sharp sand or horticultural grit.

ABOVE: The finished scheme.
RIGHT: The edges of the log roll are softened by trailing plants – *Sedum x rubrotinctum* (left) and *Crassula volkensii*.

Building brick or stone walls, again perhaps in a series of beds, will give you further hard landscaping. For major impact you can make a fabulous 'escarpment', with rockery stone built up in layers. This will give you a wonderful natural staging for all those containers, and a lot of natural-looking, but remarkably comfortable, seating. The photographs show how flexible this system is to construct: in the case illustrated, the plants are arranged in containers in the conservatory, using the rocks as staging and continuing the planting and rocks up on to the windowsill. This creates a really flexible and easily altered display, which continues outside the glass into the garden, where the rockery contains a harmonious permanent planting of hardy opuntias. The result is a real feeling of space and continuity.

A carefully planned abundance of flat surfaces allows the introduction of a variety of cacti and other succulents in pots.

Most of these are opuntias, but the eagle-eyed will spot a *Cereus jamacaru* and an *Aporocactus flagriformis*.

A bare and uninviting conservatory corner . . .

. . . on its way to being transformed into a rockery.

The conservatory rockery seems to spill out into the garden, running down a gentle slope to the path.

The view from inside, with its colourful echoes and repetitions.

## LOOKING AFTER YOUR BEDS

In all cases, you need to consider the twin problems of providing sufficient drainage and controlling pests.

In a bed dug out of the conservatory base the soil will be both poor and compacted. In this case, it's a good idea to import fresh soil mixed with a really generous amount of drainage material like horticultural grit, sharp sand or pea shingle to create a loose, open, free-draining home for your plants to thrive in.

In a raised bed, create a drainage layer of rocks, bricks or other **hard core**, extending up to a third of the depth of the bed, and then top this with a free-draining soil mixture as described above. (See below.)

As far as pest control is concerned, prevention is definitely preferable to cure, as an insect invasion is very difficult to eradicate. Make sure the plants you introduce are clean and healthy specimens. A thorough insecticiding before hand is a good precaution: do keep an eye on the bed and zap things as soon as they appear.

Before you begin planting, plan the appearance and long-term care of your bed. Spend as much time creating a miniature landscape as you would your garden planting schemes.

Cross-section of a raised bed, showing drainage layer.

Star performance: this *Aloe davyana* and the trailing plants on either side (*Portulacaria afra* 'Foliisvariegatus' and *Crassula sarmentosa* 'Variegata') spill over the log roll to give an impression of abundance.

## CHOOSING PLANTS FOR CONSERVATORY BEDS

You can have an informal mixed bed of cacti and succulents or a much more uncompromising cactus bed. In every case, try to arrange your plants to give as much variety of shape, colour and form as possible, because this sort of mass grouping can be very dramatic. You can also have permanent planting with strategic gaps for a rotation of specimens in containers. These can be popped in and out of position to ring the changes – to show off a stunning plant in flower or to accommodate plants which are either coming back inside after a summer holiday spent in the great outdoors or which, having been indoors, are ready for a vacation of their own in better-lit surroundings.

Just as you would with a garden border, plan your backdrop, your medium-height displays and your smaller **focal planting** in the front of the bed. Again, as with a garden, use some

rapid-growing temporary stock to infill while your choice subjects reach their intended size and create the impact you intend.

Eventually you can use tall columnar plants as a backdrop: cereus and opuntias amongst the cacti, for example, or some of the succulent euphorbias which have the same habit. In time you can grow a mini forest of these impressive characters. In the meantime, you could always plant rapid-growing and exotic *Yucca elephantipes* (sold as the infamous Spanish 'stick in a bag', which gives you an idea of how readily it roots and reroots) to give some impact while you wait.

The alternative approach is to create a backdrop of climbing or trailing subjects – *Sedum morganianum*, *Ceropegia woodii* or rhipsalis species such as *Rhipsalis cereuscula* or *R. salicornioides* – which will clothe trellis panels or hang from a series of containers on the wall. Hoyas such as *Hoya carnosa* will climb happily and produce waxy clusters of flowers on sinuous branches in darker corners.

You can also consider ivy, either as a temporary or permanent 'cheat', which will give you a tolerant and rapid-growing background to any of these plants, and which

Backing group: *Ceropegia woodii* makes a colourful foliage backdrop.

Home furnishings: bracts of bougainvillaea create an exotic conservatory 'wallpaper'.

will find sufficient nourishment in the bed to put on a good show for you. Passion flowers (Passiflora) are another rampant 'wallpaper', creating a rapid backdrop, and they have the added advantage of bearing exotic flowers. And there is always bougainvillaea, which will flourish in a conservatory. It is very drought-tolerant and has almost blindingly bright and prolific 'flowers' – actually colourful **bracts** – and thus gives you both a glossy, dark green leafy background and brilliant colour. Both passion flowers and bougainvillaea can be a bit messy after flowering, however, and there is a lot of clearing up to do if you don't want a litter of fallen flowers or bracts.

Other good fillers are some of the other succulent plants, like aeoniums and agaves, which will spread like triffids given a free root run, while *Portulacaria afra* will rapidly grow into a nice miniature shrub with emerald green leaves and red stems. If you simultaneously plant globular cacti they will grow into fat round plants given time, a prime example being the fabulous *Echinocactus grusonii* – also cruelly known as mother-in-law's chair – which create huge spiny yellow cushions.

You can also use lower-growing succulents to form multi-coloured carpets and to create an overhanging, living edge to your bed or border.

## WATER FEATURES

Just as in the garden, water features make an appealing addition to a conservatory, where the sight and sound of running water is wonderfully cooling in the heat of summer.

There is a good choice of tiny waterfalls, fountains and other sculptured ornaments which can be surrounded with plants for a landscaped feel. You can also get really small pumps for a very low cost, and they are not quite as worrying electrically as pumps installed outside, which need to be heavy-duty and protected from damage by the weather and by garden tools such as spades and lawn mowers. Nevertheless, unless you are completely sure of your electrical competence, do use a qualified electrical engineer to install it for you.

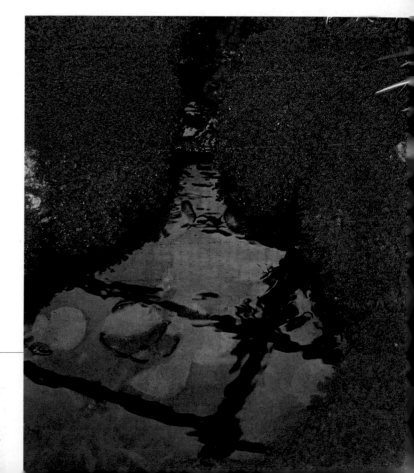

Go with the flow: the ripple and murmur of running water gives an extra dimension to a conservatory – and the stream doesn't need to be large.

Some of the features you can buy include sets of tiny bowls, the water cascading from one into another, with surrounding spaces for inserting plants. If you are going to have a situation like this, where there is splashing and the plants will be close to the water, don't use true cacti. Leafier trailing succulents, like some of those in Chapter 8, will grow more successfully.

You can also consider features such as lion heads on walls and mini millstones or pebble pools, all of which are available in the mass DIY outlets as well as in good garden and water garden centres. These are the safest option if you have children, who are inevitably drawn to water and can drown in almost no depth at all.

You may, of course, choose to have a traditional pond, although on a much smaller scale, with a cascading waterfall, one of the miniature waterlilies and even a fish or two. (One of our photographs shows how even a tiny pool can house goldfish.) There is also a more formal, ready-made structure which you can buy complete with pump, pond and fountain. Classical urn-carrying nymphs, bucolic mediaeval peasants and 'bad taste' comedy animals all have their place, and can be bought complete for the cost of a visit to the theatre with meal to follow.

The two schemes illustrated demonstrate the good and bad taste approach, and I hope they will give you some inspiration for schemes of your own. The first has an elegant, pale, classical nymph surrounded by colour-themed white and black chippings and an assortment of succulents such as aeoniums, cotyledons, and echeverias, plus white-spined cacti, all in shades of grey and purple-black.

The 'good taste' scheme uses no soil, but has a brick perimeter filled in with black and white chippings.

The area is then dressed with colour-themed cacti and other succulents in pots – here deep purple *Aeonium arboreum* 'Zwartkop' with toning echeverias and pale-spined cacti.

The second has a Mexican feel, with a big stone lizard stalking through spiky euphorbias and cacti ranging from opuntias to mammillarias. These surround a water feature, which consists of two rather smaller and more soporific lizards slurping from a giant whisky bottle. You will have to decide which version is in the best taste, although the lizards would, I'm sure, choose the whisky!

ABOVE: A layer of gravel is added for drainage, then topped with gritty compost to a total depth of around 10cm (4in). A mock stone plinth is then put in place.

RIGHT: The bed is topped up with gravel (for decoration and to stabilize the plinth) and the miniature pond, whisky fountain and attendant lizard are added.

ABOVE: The 'bad taste' scheme requires planting in soil, so engineering bricks are first placed directly on the paving slabs . . .

LEFT: . . .a waterproof membrane is then added . . .

BELOW: . . . and secured by a course of small pavers. A layer of sand prevents drainage material piercing the liner and damaging the conservatory paving.

BELOW: Finally the finished scheme is planted through the gravel and into the soil beneath.

## NOT STRICTLY FOR THE BIRDS: UNUSUAL SETTINGS

There are some other circumstances in which you may choose to use succulent plants for their practical advantages. Aviaries, reptile houses and terrariums look much more attractive if they are planted up, but the care of 'normal' plants can be extremely difficult in these environments. Reptile houses, for instance, need to be hot and dry for the benefit of their live occupants, while watering can be a tricky business in aviaries, because small birds are not only brilliant escape artists but rapidly succumb to damp and cold. Succulents are custom-made for these areas.

When we kept foreign finches, half of our conservatory was converted into an aviary for these pretty birds, which flew freely outside our living room, alighting on perches made from natural branches which we brought in. Unfortunately our original attempts to clothe the space with shrubs and flowering plants in containers was not an unmixed success. Access through double doors in order to trap escapees was never easy, and the amount of water needed created problems, the environment easily becoming too wet for the birds. For their part, the finches were also very hard on normal plants: the aviary was totally clothed with a beautiful flowering honeysuckle on one outside end of the flight, but let a single stem stray through the wire and they pulverized it instantly.

The real macaw: this scarlet beauty may be fake, but it's possible to create a succulent aviary busy with pretty finches and other exotic birds.

Once we changed to an assortment of massed planting of succulents in large containers, plus hanging baskets and a little judicious planting into the soil at the edges of the aviary, we found that the plants grew and thrived with far less watering. The birds were also much happier and a lot less bedraggled. We did need to rotate containers from time to time, to allow the plants to be cleaned up from the bird droppings, and the plants also had to be very fleshy and waxy (aeoniums, *Crassula ovata,* or agaves which have had their **terminal spines** removed with secateurs) because the birds would attack anything with more delicate leaves.

Ivy, mentioned above as a useful backdrop, also has a place here, in that the birds won't spoil it – indeed, ours enjoyed roosting amongst the leaves which clothed the wall. We also trained ivy over the otherwise bare perches (from which even the bark had gone), and we had leafy 'trees' which seemed to be bird-proof.

There is, therefore, a wonderful symbiosis in growing succulent and drought-resistant plants to decorate and beautify spaces which would otherwise be impossible to manage. Don't, however, be tempted to put spiny cacti in with your pets. In the glasshouse at the nursery we had a stray blackbird which became impaled on the fish hook-like spines of a huge mammillaria. Bleeding and panic-stricken, it had to be extricated hook by hook, and we were never sure if the poor thing would survive the blood loss and terror once it flew free again.

Flight path: agaves and aeoniums are too tough to be eaten by small birds, which will enjoy the hot, dry conditions in which succulents thrive. The agaves must have their spines removed.

# CHAPTER 4
# CARE AND MAINTENANCE

The good news for succulent growers with a busy life is that your plants
will prefer benign neglect to over-zealous attention

Easy does it: cacti and other succulents require only the minimum of care in order to look as good as this. Left to right: *Echeveria setosa*, *Cotyledon undulata*, *Crassula falcata*, *Echeveria runyonii* 'Topsy-turvy' and *Aeonium domesticum* 'Variegatum'

Although these are easy plants to care for, you need to cultivate a hard heart if your plants are to really thrive. Forget all your preconceptions: traditionally, house and conservatory plants are a constant worry, regarded as always in need of water, food or both. We are instructed to keep a moist microclimate around the plants by standing them in trays filled with pebbles and water in order to create a constant humidity, and the last thing we should ever do is let the compost dry out completely. If a plant wilts, its condition is often terminal, so a sickly plant is generally treated with water – and that means lots of it.

Now, however, you must forget all of those rules. Cacti and the other succulents are more likely to die from over-zealous care than for any other reason, so you will need to develop a culture of benign neglect. Don't worry even if your plants appear to shrivel slightly: they will be magically resurrected as soon as they receive water.

## COMPOSTS

Succulents will thrive in any normal house-plant compost, either multipurpose mixes or John Innes soil-based compost, numbers 2 or 3. Soilless multipurpose composts are lightweight, so you may find that pots containing taller plants will topple over when

Hung over: a mammillaria rotting from the inside out – a consequence of too much water, too much cold, or both.

they are due to be watered. The advantage of this compost, however, is that you can easily knock the root ball out of the pot to examine the root system for pests, and the whole plant can be turned out and put back into its pot without any mess or compost loss. Soil-based composts are heavier, so your pots will remain more stable, but if you turn invert the pot all the compost will cascade out and the plant will need repotting. If you suspect that you will be heavy-handed with watering, add horticultural grit to the mix to improve drainage – although in this case you will have a landslide when you come to upend the pot, whichever compost you use.

All of these plants should be completely dry before they are next watered. Don't, however, go to the opposite extreme of potting your plants in sand and neglecting to water them at all. True, they won't die, but they certainly won't look very attractive, either.

Once the compost is dry, the plants should be given a generous drenching and then allowed to dry out again. You will find that the plants are being watered once a week in the summer, possibly twice if it is very

sunny. However, if you are in any doubt about watering, *don't*. The plants won't suffer, and it is safer to water too little than too much. Although containers can look very pretty with a top dressing of gravel, this does mean that you can't tell whether the compost has dried out or not: until you are used to succulents, keep at least one or two pots free of top-dressing so that you can check on their condition more easily.

When the plants are in full growth they appreciate regular feeding every four weeks or so. There are special formulations for cacti, such as Chempak cactus and succulent fertilizer, which has a specially balanced NPK (nitrogen, phosphorus, potassium) formulation of 8-34-32. Having said this, you'll find that high potassium fertilizers also suit cacti and other succulents: 15-15-30, perhaps, or similar fertilizers formulated for tomatoes, such as NPK 10-10-25 or 11-9-30. A balanced NPK will do no harm, however, so the most indolent solution is to mix a little granulated slow release fertilizer with a 20-20-20 formulation into the compost when you first pot up the plants.

Beating the bugs: this *Echeveria setosa* is infested with root mealy bugs, and needs a dose of insecticide, after which its compost should be replaced (see p. 52).

## WHEN TO WATER

You can grow a very wide range of plants in either an unheated or in a frost-free conservatory as long as the plants are completely dry over the winter. An unheated conservatory is often effectively the same as one which will be kept just above freezing (about 4°C, or 40°F), because the borrowed heat from the house is usually enough to keep the temperature that bit higher than it would be in a freestanding greenhouse.

In the autumn gradually reduce watering until, by November, your plants are completely dry. They will then stay bone-dry until the spring when, from March onwards, watering very gradually starts up again to bring the plants back into growth. This is the most critical stage for cacti, as too much water too soon may cause them to rot, so let the pot dry out completely between waterings. You will be able to see when the plants are making new growth: in a globular cactus, for example, a tightly packed fur of new spines appears in the growing point or points of the plants, and the whole plant becomes plumper.

This dry period is necessary in order to protect the plants during the winter. If you look at photographs of the same plants taken at different times you will see that the plants are literally smaller in the winter, shrunk into themselves to protect their structures. This **dormancy** is also essential for bud formation, and a failure to provide it is the commonest reason for flowering to fail. Once your plants have reached the necessary size they should flower like clockwork every year, as long as they have had their winter snooze. They generally flower in the spring or early summer. The rebutias, mammillarias, lobivias, notocactus, epiphyllums (orchid cacti) and Christmas cacti are particularly good for flowers, and some will bloom more than once in the same year.

The treatment of your cacti and other succulents indoors or in a heated conservatory is necessarily rather different. The plants still need to have a drier resting period, but they won't go into the kind of suspended animation that they would adopt in the colder conditions of a space kept just above freezing. In warmer conditions you will need to give your plants an occasional light watering or misting from time to time to prevent them shrivelling. This applies especially to the other succulents, which may well carry on growing, although more slowly, throughout the winter. Some of the crassulas will also delight you with masses of tiny white flowers – very welcome in the winter months. Keep all cacti (except Christmas

Drink problem: this echeveria attacked by mould is a sorry victim of overwatering.

Winter wonder: well-tended crassulas will often reward you with a mass of tiny white flowers in what is generally a barren time of the year.

It is, however, safe to remove them if you would prefer a tidier plant. Just wait until they are completely dead and dry, when you can rub them away.

Unfortunately, in an artificial environment like a conservatory you cannot rely on the normal checks and balances to keep pests under control, so you will need to keep your eyes open for insect pests. On the whole, plants that are well looked after are much less susceptible to attack. Luckily, you won't find masses of blackfly, greenfly or whitefly disfiguring your plants (except possibly your aeoniums), because these plants don't have the soft leaves which aphids love.

cacti) as dry as possible, with a light watering if they appear too **dessicated**. The other succulents require similar care although, in general, they need less sun and a little more water, and they are rather more vigorous in their growth. Lithops are the notable exception, relishing a sunny position and hating too much water.

Cacti and other succulents make attractive all-year-round houseplants because you will find that their appearance won't change very much during the colder months.

## HYGIENE

Basic hygiene, both in the house and the conservatory, involves removing dead leaves and the debris of flowers and other material which gathers around the pots: this helps avoid fungal infection. You can leave flowers on, in which case they often form attractive and colourful seed pods and will possibly give you your own seed to experiment with.

Feeding time: a ladybird enjoying a meal of whitefly. Fortunately aeoniums are the only succulents susceptible to aphid attack.

## PESTS AND DISEASES

### MEALY BUGS
(*Pseudococcus* species)

These look a bit like woodlice in shape, but they have a protective waxy white coating, so you will see these as white, woolly tufts, about 1–3mm (¹/₁₂in) long, which are tucked into inaccessible corners of leaf joints, camouflaged in the wool around spines and so on. These are generally slow-moving, sucking parasites which can be removed individually in a small infestation by dabbing them with methylated spirits on a cotton wool bud. Larger infestations need treatment with either a **systemic insecticide** such as dimethoate (sold as Murphy's systemic), a broad spectrum insecticide containing pirimiphos-methyl, such as Sybol, or one of the malathion-based insecticides. Although malathion has a low level of toxicity to mammals, it is worth bearing in mind that it is deadly to bees.

### ROOT MEALY BUGS
(*Rhizoecus* species)

These are a much greater pest, because they are completely hidden from view while feasting on the roots, causing stunting or failure of the plant. For this reason you will need to turn the plant out of the pot from time to time to check for tell-tale white tufts amongst the roots and compost. This is the argument for a soilless multipurpose compost, because you can examine the root ball and pop the plant straight back into its pot without having to repot it. You can use the same cotton wool remedy as above, but there is a case for removing compost from the roots, dunking the plant in insecticide and repotting it in fresh compost. Malathion or a systemic insecticide can be used.

### SCALE INSECTS
(*Dactylopius cacti*)

These can be cactus lovers: indeed, they are grown commercially on Opuntias for

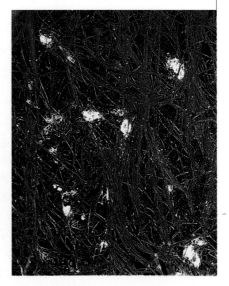

Alien invasions: mealy bugs nesting on a *Crassula lactea* leaf (left) and a *Cereus* (below left); and root mealy bugs infesting *Echeveria setosa (below right)*.

A mite unhealthy: this dark-bodied neoporteria shows typical damage inflicted by sap-sucking red spider mites.

cochineal, the red dye. (There are other culprits, such as *Pinnaspis aspidistrae* and *Coccus hesperidum*.) They can be seen as small spots about 2–6mm ($^1/_{16}$–$^1/_4$in) in diameter, which cling on in a limpet-like manner: these are the females, which have a protective shell to protect them while they suck sap and lay their eggs. Low-grade infestations can be treated with methylated spirits or soapy water on a cotton bud or paintbrush. Otherwise use malathion or Sybol.

### SAP-SUCKING RED SPIDER MITES
(*Tetranychus* species)
Almost invisible to the naked eye, they are about 0.02mm ($^1/_{000}$in) across and usually look like tiny orange dots, though they can be other colours, and they are always surrounded with a very fine webbing. Treatment must be rapid, as this is a pest which can spread quickly. These bugs are susceptible to insecticides containing butoxycarboxim. If you dislike chemical treatments, you can mist the plants and open windows as a deterrent, because this is a bug of dry conditions and poor ventilation. You can also use Neem tree oil as described in the panel on the right.

### SCIARID FLY (*Sciaridae*)
A pest of wet, peat-based compost, the sciarid fly is a problem especially when seedlings are being raised, so these bugs are dealt with under propagation in Chapter 3.

### CHEMICAL-FREE CONTROL
If you are unhappy about the use of toxic chemicals in close proximity to your living space, you may be interested in some new research into the use of diatomaceous earth, which is made from the skeletal remains of minute algae. Traditionally used in water filtration processes, this completely inert material can be used at a rate of a tablespoon to a litre of soil. It destroys mealy bugs in an elegant, if gruesome, manner: the remains of the algae are reduced to needle-sharp particles which are believed to shred the bodies of small soil-inhabiting insects.

There is also a non-toxic, biodegradable substance derived from the oil of the Neem tree (*Azadirachta indica*), a native of Burma and India where it is traditionally known as 'the village pharmacy'. Neem tree oil is non-toxic and biodegradable and is believed to have insecticidal and fungicidal properties. It is used in a solution of one ounce (30mls) of oil to a gallon (4.5 litres) of water, together with an equal amount of soft soap.

If you can bring yourself to live with plants which are not entirely pest free, then you might try to achieve a natural balance by using biological controls. Ladybirds will attack mealy bugs and scale insects, while syrphid flies and lacewings live on mealy bugs.

LEFT: Vine weevil larvae (actual size), and the damage they have done to an echeveria.

## DEADLY COMPOST

Since there are obvious reservations about spraying insecticides in a living area, you may like to consider a new method of pest control. Levington has produced Houseplant Protection Compost, which incorporates the insecticide Intercept (imidacloprid). Not an organo-phosphate, this can knock out some insects resistant to other pesticides without affecting predatory insects such as ladybirds. It will control soil-dwelling pests for a year and, because it is also systemic, it additionally controls pests of the above-ground plant such as the leaf mealy bug.

There are disadvantages. The compost must not be diluted or bulked out and, as the insecticide cannot move from treated to untreated compost, you must remove all your existing compost first. Plants which are already infested must, therefore, have all the soil removed from the root ball, and the plant root system should be flushed with clean water before potting up in the new protective compost.

Intercept is also now available as a liquid insecticide, Provado Vine Weevil Killer by Bio which, despite its name, also attacks root mealy bug.

LEFT: The burrow of a leaf cutter bee can clearly be seen among the roots of this *Alworthia bicarinata*

LEFT: The fungal infection damaging this echinopsis has been caused by the secretions of mealy bugs.

LEFT: An echeveria attacked by mould.

BELOW LEFT: Rot can spread to kill the leaf and even the whole plant – here an aloe.

BELOW: This aloe has 'die-back' at the leaf tips, caused by excessive dryness.

## FUNGAL INFECTION

This is often an indicator of poor hygiene, because these condition will only develop in the kind of damp conditions to which cacti

and other succulents should never be subjected. However, you can treat infected plants with a proprietary copper-based **fungicide** or with Benlate.

## REPOTTING

As your plants grow and change they will need to be moved into larger containers, with fresh nutrient-rich compost and room for the roots to spread. With most of your plants this is straightforward. Choose a clean pot, the next size up from the one your plant is in, fill it loosely with compost and push the smaller pot down into it to make an outline of the space the root ball will need. Dislodge the plant from the container by turning it upside down and tapping it sharply on the side of a bench, shelf or table.

Take this opportunity to have a really good look at the root ball, to make sure that there is no damage or infestation. If you find mealy bugs, remove all the compost from the roots and dispose of it well away from other plants. Dip the plant in an insecticide such as malathion or Sybol before potting the plant up in clean, new compost. Take a look at the plants surrounding the infested one in case the pests have begun to spread. If this is the case, it is important to give those plants a dose of insecticide, too.

Nice, clean plants may simply have the stale compost teased from around their roots, with the plant being dropped into the pot while new compost is gently firmed in around it. Let the plant settle in its new home for a day or two, and then start watering again, beginning with lower quantities than normal until the plant has had time to recover.

## SAFETY

You may be baffled when you look at a really prickly cactus, wondering how you can put it into a larger pot without danger of harm to yourself. Damage limitation methods include the obvious one of wearing stout gloves. You may, however, be surprised how spines can penetrate even the toughest material.

There is another, cunning alternative approach which avoids damage to you or the plant. Take a page of newspaper and fold it over and over until it makes a firm, long, thin rectangular strip. Put this around the plant, and pinch the two ends of the strip together with your finger and thumb, close to the plant body, creating a handle to hold. You will find that you will have a circular collar surrounding the plant, which you can hold gently but firmly enough for you to be able to upend the pot and tap it to loosen the plant as described above. Still using your handle, you can place the plant in its new container and firm it in with no harm to either of you. (See below.)

Children are often fascinated by cacti, yet the spines can be fierce and some have a horrible fish-hook feature, so it is easy for little fingers – and pets' noses – to get damaged. If you have children or pets, therefore, do please keep your spikiest plants, such as the cacti and some of the agaves with their terminal spines, well out of their reach. The agave spines can also be cut off, using scissors or secateurs, with no harm whatsoever to the plant.

Safety first: a handle made of newspaper keeps sharp spines at bay.

# CHAPTER 5
# PLANTS
# FOR FREE

Propagating your plants from cuttings, offsets
and self-collected seed allows you to amass a
sizeable collection with no extra outlay

Something for nothing: even filling a small windowsill can be a challenge, but this euphorbia (centre) is very easy to propagate from a cutting or to grow from seed.

The prospect of filling a single windowsill, let alone the aching vastness of a new and empty conservatory, with enough plants to make a really good display can seem a very daunting one. The process threatens to be mind-numbingly slow, and yet the expense of buying every single plant is prohibitive.

One of the big bonuses of any kind of gardening, however, is **propagating** extra plants of your own at little or no cost. By using your existing plants as material to be cannibalized, you can make an impact on those blank spaces much more rapidly than you perhaps imagined.

Cacti and succulents give the opportunity for a variety of approaches, from taking offsets and cuttings, through grafting, to growing plants from your own seed.

## OFFSETS

Fortunately the clustering cacti will reproduce themselves in miniature as part of their normal habit of growth, and these offsets are perfect replicas of the parent plant. You can, of course, allow the original to grow on and develop into a wonderful multi-headed specimen. However, in the summer months when the plant is growing so vigorously that both the parent and its offsets will recover rapidly, you can choose to take some or all of the babies away from the

An offset of *Mammillaria zeilmanniana* with roots developing.

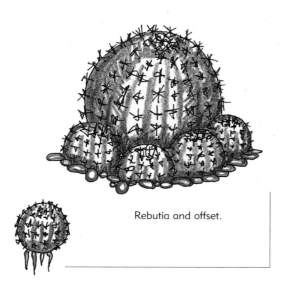

Rebutia and offset.

Agave and offset in the compost (above). Offset on its own (above right).

parent, potting them on to grow into larger plants. The extra space and nourishment now available to the mother plant means it will grow more quickly than if left intact.

Many of the globular cacti, such as rebutias, echinopsis, chamaecereus, lobivias and mammillarias, are freely **offsetting**, and even some of the rarer genera will often clump up readily, too. Notocactus are unusual in that, although they offset readily, they often reproduce underground. To find the offsets, probe through the soil gently with your finger tips until you find their hiding places.

You may find that once you have turned the plant out of its pot, you can separate the offsets by tugging them gently apart. If you are lucky you will also find you have a tiny root system, in which case you can immediately pot up the 'pup' into any houseplant compost. You have a choice between John Innes soil-based compost (numbers 1 or 2), a peat-based compost, which will benefit from the addition of a little gravel, or any of the new, coir-based or multipurpose variants, again with the addition of a little gravel.

Sometimes you have to be more ruthless and cut the offset away from the parent with a clean, sharp knife. Put the offset to one side

in a dry, shady place for the cut surface to callous over. This will take about a week or ten days, and then you can pot the plant up in the same mixture as for the ready-rooted offset described above.

Any of the readily clumping and clustering succulents, such as faucarias, lithops, and conophytums, can be treated in the same way. Separate them gently, just as with the cacti. If they have been cut you will need to wait a week or ten days, but otherwise you can pot them up straight away.

Some succulents, like agaves and aloes, produce offsets on thickened runners which develop in the root system. You will find these baby plants appearing around and under the rosettes, although you can also often find them under the surface when you are repotting the plants. A bowl or cauldron-shaped container with curved sides is good for these plants as it seems to encourage the offsets to head to the surface quickly. These baby plants can be detached gently from the parent plant and potted up immediately, because they already have their own root systems.

LEFT: Stapelia and stem cutting.

RIGHT: Chamaecereus and cutting.

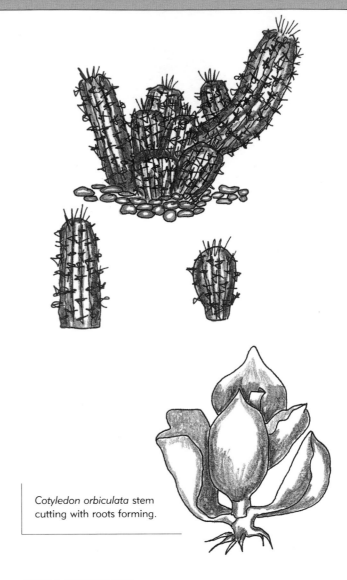

Cotyledon orbiculata stem cutting with roots forming.

## CUTTINGS

Because some plants are much less obliging, you will have to take things into your own hands if you want to produce extra plants as quickly as you can. Your cuttings should be taken during the growing season. Late spring and early summer are the best time, and all propagation is best done between early spring and early autumn. It is certainly possible to take cuttings in the autumn, but in this case they are best left unpotted until the following spring: if they are in a dry position they will amaze you with their ability to survive in a kind of suspended animation, and when you eventually come to pot them up you may well find that roots are already beginning to form.

An essential tool when taking cuttings is a clean, sharp, preferably unserrated knife. You also need some clean, dry, empty plant saucers or seed trays, in which you can place the cut material in a dry and shaded position while it dries out. Hygiene is essential. Dirt and moisture harbour all sorts of moulds, bacteria and pests which might infect your plant material. Ideally you should also thoroughly clean the blade between each cutting to prevent the spread of infection.

### STEM CUTTINGS

Taking stem cuttings is a form of **vegetative propagation**. The plants that you grow from the cuttings will be identical to the parents, and this can be vital if some feature, such as **variegation**, cannot be perpetuated in any other way. Interestingly, variegation in a plant cannot be reproduced by leaf cuttings: there has to be some stem involved or the plant will be the self-green of the original species again.

Cuttings should be taken at a natural joint if possible – from the side or base in the case of a branching cactus, or a stem or pad in a jointed species. Most cacti and many fleshy-stemmed succulents can be propagated like this.

Off with its head: an *Opuntia subulata* before and after execution. The lower part will often sprout to form a majestic candelabrum.

This is also a good way to increase some of the exotic flowering cacti, like epiphyllums, aporocactus and selenicereus, all of which root readily as stem cuttings. However, if you cut the stem into several pieces, do remember to mark which end is the bottom: it is often hard to tell which end is which, but it is really important to pot them up the right way in the compost.

Take great care with euphorbia cuttings, as all of these plants have a milky and irritant sap. If you begin taking your cuttings from the bottom of the plant and work your way upwards you can avoid a lot of trouble, because this way the sap will not drip on you as you continue to take your cuttings. Watering the stock plant afterwards will remove most of the white sap. I would suggest that you always wear gloves with euphorbias, and that you wash your hands well after taking cuttings of *any* plant.

It may sound ruthless, but you can take your cutting straight across a stem. The plant will look very sorry for itself, but the top part can be rooted to form a perfect new plant and the cut surface will sprout several new pieces which can be detached in turn to make new plants or left where they are so that they produce a branching plant. *Opuntia subulata* and other **columnar** plants such as cereus and cleistocactus can be treated like this, and the resulting parent plant can become a really striking candelabrum in time. In the case of padded opuntias you can remove a pad (again, this will trigger the parent to produce more than one pad to replace it) or you can take off a side branch.

As well as increasing your stock, taking cuttings is a way of managing plants. Cuttings can be used to rescue a diseased plant if you cut off a healthy part well above the diseased or damaged section. You can also tidy up a lopsided or top-heavy growth, or behead a columnar plant that is outgrowing its space; a new, smaller plant will be established, while the cut portion will resprout into a more compact multi-headed plant. A cutting will often grow away with much more vigour than the parent plant, which may have been slowing down.

Take a bit of time before you start sawing away at your plants. Look for the most suitable area to separate the cutting from the host plant, and make it a smooth, even cut, with no rough edges. Put the cutting in a clean container in a dry, shady place – perhaps tucked under a conservatory shelf – where it should remain to dry out for a week or so, erring on the side of more rather than less time. Its progress depends on both the temperature and time of the year, as a cutting will be ready sooner in the middle of the growing season and when temperatures are higher. This isn't rocket science, however, and you won't court certain failure if you pot a cutting up a bit too soon. If you are really worried, just wait until you see the tiny new roots appearing: pot your cutting up at this point, and success is virtually guaranteed.

You may be experienced at taking cuttings of 'normal' house and garden plants, but remember that, unlike most other plants, cacti actually dislike being too wet. These are the last plants to root up by standing them in a glass of water. Because cacti and other succulents lack the resistance to bacteria and moisture-borne fungal infections which plants originating in wetter areas possess, they fall prey to these attacks very readily. Keep them dry, and they will often surprise you by producing tiny roots even before you come to pot them up.

After a week or two, pot them up into slightly moist compost. Any house plant compost will do (multipurpose, peat-based with extra gravel or soil-based), but they will appreciate a gritty mix, which you can give them by adding a generous handful of horticultural grit or sharp sand – just think how quickly weed seedlings will root in garden gravel beds which have no weed suppression membrane in place. Water the cuttings really sparingly until they show signs of growth, when you can build up watering until you are giving them water and feed as usual.

LEAF CUTTINGS

Many succulents, among them echeverias, crassulas, kalanchoes and sedums, can be propagated quickly and easily by removing a leaf from the parent plant. Choose a plump healthy leaf and allow it to dry out, just as with the stem cuttings. You will find that a whole new miniature plant will develop from the base of the leaf, which will eventually shrivel away.

**Rosette**-forming succulents can be set with a small piece of stem still attached. Aeoniums can be propagated by taking one of the rosettes which form its crown.

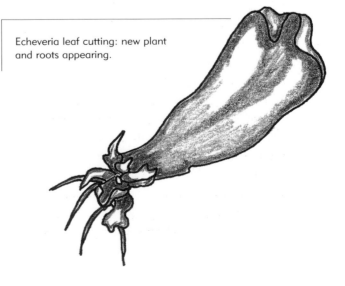

Echeveria leaf cutting: new plant and roots appearing.

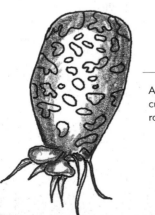

Adromischus leaf cutting: plant and roots forming.

A root cutting of yucca, with new plants developing.

## ROOT CUTTINGS

If you look at the root system of yuccas and agaves you will sometimes see a very thick branching which is distinctly different from the normal, thinner and more fibrous appearance. Cut off pieces of this engorged root, allowing the sections to dry out, and you will be rewarded with a new crop of plants. The pieces should be at least 5cm (2in) long, and they should preferably have some small roots on them already. With time, complete new plantlets will form from these pieces, sometimes with the additional bonus of more than one per section. Once a plantlet has developed its own roots, cut it off the parent root, pot it up in the usual mixture and then gradually build up your watering regime as before.

## COLLECTING YOUR OWN SEED

Many of the cacti genera make a dazzling display of flowers in the spring and early summer, and then go on to set seed, while some other succulents, such as the autumn-flowering lithops, will also set seed readily. Keep an eye on the ripening pods, which should be removed from the plant once they are ripe and the mature seed is black and hard. Our motto should always be: the fresher the seed the better. To remove the seedpods is also to practise good hygiene, because those left on over the winter are not only a focus for rot and decay, but they are also all too susceptible to raids by hungry mice. Having said that, however, plants such as mammillarias and rhipsalis have such pretty fruits that aesthetics can sometimes outweigh good housekeeping.

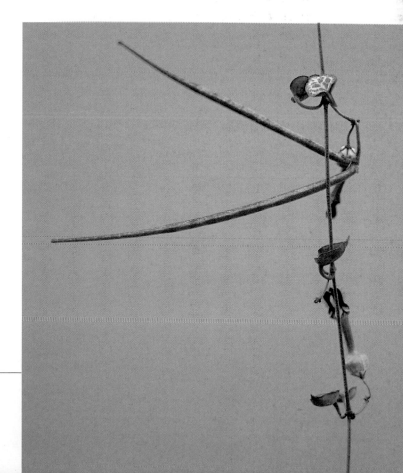

Ripening: these highly attractive seed pods of *Ceropegia woodii* will soon be ready to remove from the plant.

Abundant new life: *Setiechinopsis mirabilis*
freshly in bud (above) . . .

. . . with the bud well-developed (left),
and with a packed seed pod which has
just burst open.

Pods of some species will split open readily, and the ripe seed will cascade out ready for sowing. Rebutias will flower readily in the spring, will quickly fruit and will provide you with ripe seed which you can have germinating by mid-summer.

Some of the seed pods, such as mammillarias, are fleshy. To remove this seed, squash the pod, then soak it well in a jar of water. You will be able to see the heavier seed separate from the pulp, dropping to the base of the container while the debris floats above it. Lithops have seemingly impenetrable seedpods, and can fox attempts to get into them. The trick here is to give them literally a drop of water, and the pods will peel open magically to reveal a really fine, dust-like seed. Don't sneeze!

Of course, some species will hybridize very readily. This can be exciting with, say, epiphyllum or chamaecereus, which may give you your own choice **hybrid** with a

Fruitful: *Mammilaria
bombycina* with ripe
seedpods ready for
harvesting.

fabulous flower colouration. You can control the outcome by selecting likely parents. Epiphyllum growers have produced a cornucopia of beautifully coloured hybrids by this method. There is also scope with some of the other small, easily flowering globular cacti, like rebutias and sulcorebutias, and these include inter-genera hybrids such as crosses between lobivia and echinopsis.

If, on the other hand, you want your new plants to be true to the parent you need to stop insects from reaching the flowers. Use a new, clean paintbrush to cross-pollinate those you have chosen, and, to ensure that no intruder sabotages your work, put a polythene bag over each one after pollination. Hold it in place with an elastic band around the mouth, and make sure to label it with the details of its 'father', especially when you are trying to produce interesting crosses.

SEEDLING DEVELOPMENT
It is very exciting to watch the development of your seedlings from tiny beginnings to the day that they come into flower. If you are lucky this will take about 18 months, but two or three years is more usual and some types will take even longer. Sow your seed in spring or summer, unless you have access to a lighted and heated **propagator** – in which case you can set them at any time.

Stages of seedling development.

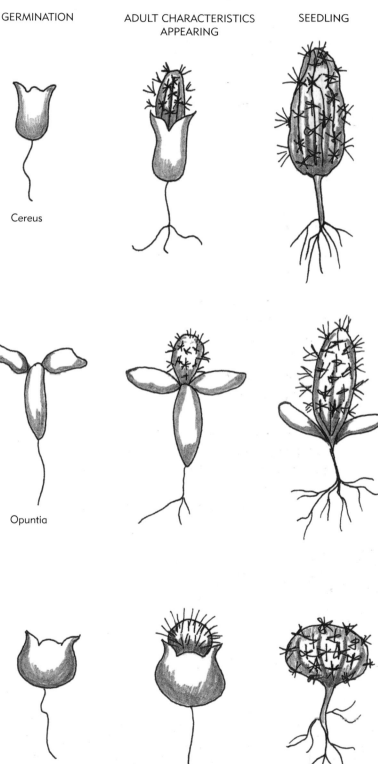

GERMINATION    ADULT CHARACTERISTICS APPEARING    SEEDLING

Cereus

Opuntia

Notocactus

Ready for sowing 1: cacti and succulent seeds vary enormously, like the plants themselves. Here we see opuntia species and *Delosperma hirtum* seeds. Both are actual size.

## SEED-RAISING

We have tried many methods of seed-raising at the nursery, and the following comes out tops. Use new, clean plastic pots, about 7.5cm (3in) in diameter, for your sowings. Loosely fill them, almost to the top, with a John Innes soil-based seed compost. Use a fine sieve to sprinkle on the final 0.5cm (¼inch) of compost, to give this layer a really open texture.

Using a sprayer, or a watering can with a fine rose, water the pot until all the compost is wet. Allow a few seconds between waterings so the water has time to sink in and doesn't wash the compost out of the pot. Alternatively soak the pots by standing them in a container of water, as illustrated on the opposite page (bottom left). After it settles, you will find that the compost will be a short distance below the top of the pot. Insert a plastic label in the middle of the pot so that it protrudes a good way above the top.

Sprinkle your seeds evenly over the surface of the compost. If you have a sprayer available (a small hand-type is ideal), wet the seeds with a fine spray of water. Despite the drought resistance of these plants, be aware that germination cannot take place unless the compost remains moist. For added protection a fungicide such as Benlate may be added to the spray. Cover the top of the pot with a transparent polythene sandwich bag, and secure it with an elastic band around the rim of the pot. The label will prevent the bag from collapsing on to the seeds.

The seedlings need protection in their first, most vulnerable weeks when they are susceptible to attack by **sciarid fly**, fungus gnats or mushroom flies – which are the same as the ubiquitous fruit flies which plague your wine glass or fruit bowl in the summer. These nuisances don't normally cause much of a problem, because they feed on decaying organic debris, but they will certainly damage tiny seedlings. Adult flies can be trapped by hanging up one of those yellow sticky flypaper strips, but this is not much help when the maggots are already there, sealed in a polythene bag with your seedlings. You can use a simple spray, like a

Ready for sowing 2: a heap of seed-raising mix (2 parts John Innes seed compost; 1 part sharp fine gravel; 1 part sharp sand) together with the equipment needed for the job – hand sprayer, pots, sieve, tray for pots, polythene bags and plant labels.

Baby Bio houseplant spray or Bio Flydown, or you can water the soil with Hexyl before setting the seeds. However, there shouldn't be a problem as long as you keep the bag in position and make absolutely sure that you have avoided using a peat-based compost, since this is a particularly good medium for these pests to thrive in.

A new product, with great potential, (as described more fully on page 54), is Levington Houseplant Protection Compost containing Intercept, a new non organo-phosphate insecticide which will control sciarid fly for a year.

Wet, wet, wet: the first task is to fill the pots and soak the compost all the way through.

Sowing time: once the labels have been pushed into the compost, the seeds are sown (small ones on top, larger ones to their own depth) and a hand sprayer is used to soak the seeds – either with plain water or with a fungicide mix.

Place the pot in a warm place – a temperature of about 20°C (70°F) is ideal, though some fluctuation in temperature (plus or minus 5° or 6°C; 10°F) will do no harm. Darkness is not required for germination, and the best position for the seeds will be well lit but out of intense sunlight. If the light is strong, cover your pot and polythene bag with a sheet of newspaper laid loosely over the top. Intense sunlight will make your seedlings go red, and their rate of growth will be greatly reduced. If the only warm place available to you is the airing cupboard then by all means use that, although you must be prepared for germination to be less successful. Give the seedlings light as soon as they have germinated.

What you are doing is giving the seeds the environment they would enjoy in their natural habitat, where they germinate against the base of the parent plant, shaded from the worst of the sun in the moistest position. Even if you don't bother to set seeds, you will sometimes find little seedlings appearing of their own accord under, say, the fat-bellied shelter of a globular cactus in one of your pots – an interesting illustration of their natural behaviour in the wild.

After germination a temperature of 10°C (50°F) is required, but 20°C (70°F) or more will produce faster growth. Ideally, the seedlings should be left in their bags for about two months, and during this time the compost should remain moist. If it does dry out, stand the pot in a container of water until the top of the compost is wet again. It is very important, however, to check the bags regularly: if there are any problems with moss, fungal growth or stretching of the seedlings towards the light, the seedlings will be safer with the bags removed. After the polythene bags have been discarded, keep the compost slightly moist either by standing the pots in a tray of water for a few minutes or by gentle spraying from above.

Micro climate: the pots are covered with polythene bags secured with elastic bands, the central label preventing the bag from collapsing on to the seeds.

Growing up: at six months these seedlings are well advanced – rebutia species in the foreground and echinocereus at the back.

Off on their own: the Lithops seedlings seen grouped together (inset) after four months, are first transplanted (left, actual size) after about 18 months.

Once the seedlings show spines they can be **pricked out**, but this is best left for a year after sowing unless there is severe overcrowding or some other problem arises. Mild overcrowding seems to have no detrimental effects: indeed, it is probably beneficial to the development of the seedlings, perhaps because it creates a favourable microclimate. If you prick them out too soon their growth seems to slow down dramatically. Don't prick out seedlings after late summer: it is far better to wait until the late spring of the following year. In the autumn gradually reduce watering and keep the seedlings dry from late autumn until early spring. Gentle watering may be resumed after this. During the winter keep the plants in a well-lit position and don't allow their temperature to fall below about

5°C (40°F). Although some seedlings will stand lower temperatures, experimentation can be dangerous.

Once your seedlings have started into growth in the spring that follows sowing, you can feel confident that they will reach maturity.

Downy growth: these large and healthy seedlings of *Setiechinopsis mirabilis* are well on their way to maturity.

Wild thing: cristate and monstrous plants often grow much more vigorously when rooted on to a stronger growing stock, as is the case with this fine *Myrtillocactus geometrizans* var. *monstrosus*.

composite grafted plant, or it can be taken off the stock plant and treated as a cutting when it has grown big enough. This technique is also used to rescue a damaged or diseased specimen, which can often be saved by grafting a healthy part on to a stock plant.

Grafting also allows the growing of forms not found in nature. The Japanese, for example, have spent many years developing a range of gymnocalyciums without chlorophyll in shades of pinks, creams and maroons. These oddities would not stand a chance of growing if they were not grafted on a green stock for chlorophyll production.

Best of friends: red *Gymnocalycium damsii* grafted on trichocereus stock.

## GRAFTING

**Grafting** is a more complicated method of plant propagation, and an operation for the more enthusiastic grower, but it is an engrossing process and can be a useful technique for a variety of reasons.

Some cacti, especially the rare and choice varieties like aztekium, pelecyphora and blossfeldia, are very slow-growing and can take an excessively long time to reach maturity if grown on their own roots. Grafting them as seedlings can accelerate their growth. The grafted plant is likely to become more engorged, and it will often produce many offsets. It can be left indefinitely to grow as a

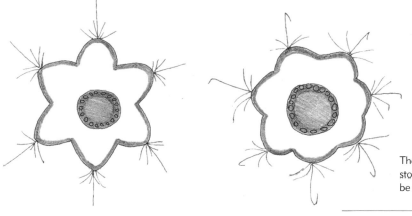

The cut surfaces of the scion and trichocereus stock, and the vascular tissue which needs to be aligned.

The unusual wavy and crested forms of cristate plants, which have developed as a result of physical, viral or genetic damage to the growing point, fascinate many people and often grow better when grafted. Some people also use this technique to create a 'standard' Christmas cactus, in the way that gardeners produce standard roses.

The best time for grafting is when plants are in strong growth, and once again the late spring and early summer is the most favoured time for trying this technique.

Success rates can be lower than in other methods of propagation, so it is probably wise to try to take several grafts at the same time in the hope that at least a few of them will prove to be successful.

The **scion** is the cutting or seedling which is to be grafted, and the vigorous rooted host plant is called the **stock**. A cactus plant obtains food and nutrients through **vascular tissue**: this can be seen in cross-section when a cactus stem is sliced through. It looks like a slightly darker core in the centre of the stem, surrounded by a circle of cells which act as water-storing tissue. For a graft to take, the vascular tissue in both the stock and scion has to be in contact in at least one place: the larger the areas in contact, the more successful the graft is likely to be. Ideally the stock plant should be a sturdy, fast-growing cactus, such

as trichocereus or pereskia. A youngish plant, a year or so old, is the best choice as this will be at its most vigorous, and the stock should be at least as wide or ideally a little bit wider than the scion. Again, you should aim for absolute cleanliness, using a clean sharp knife, and cleaning it between operations.

In **flat grafting** both the stock and the scion should be cut straight across in a clean cut, with the edges of both pieces **chamfered** to fit together so as to avoid shrinkage.

Foster mother: *Pereskia aculeata* is commonly used for grafting seedlings.

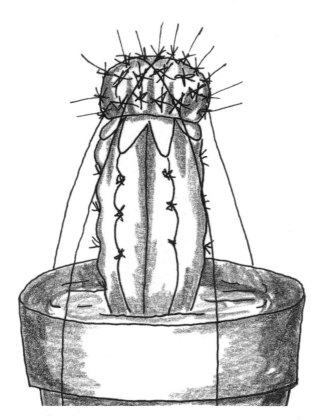

Hard graft: the trichocereus stock is chamfered to make a close fit with a gymnocalycium. Elastic bands hold the graft in place.

In the case of long, slender scions – as, for example, when you are grafting a thin, columnar cactus – use a **diagonal graft**. The stock and the scion are cut on the diagonal and married together, joining them across the maximum possible surface area.

Keep the pot in a bright position, but out of full sun, for two or three weeks, after which the graft should have taken and the bands can be removed. Protect from full sun until the scion shows obvious signs of growth, when the plant can be treated just like any other member of your collection.

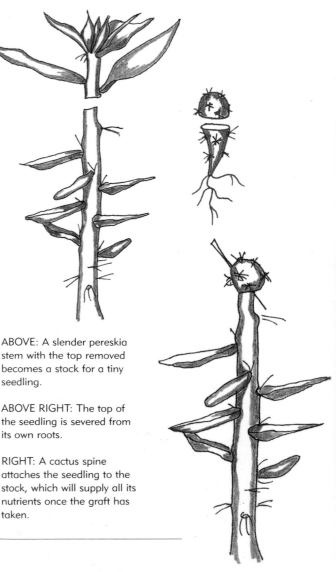

ABOVE: A slender pereskia stem with the top removed becomes a stock for a tiny seedling.

ABOVE RIGHT: The top of the seedling is severed from its own roots.

RIGHT: A cactus spine attaches the seedling to the stock, which will supply all its nutrients once the graft has taken.

Look carefully at the stock and the scion for the vascular rings. These should be lined up as far as possible, because this it where the plants will bond together. Try to avoid any air bubbles becoming trapped between the two cut sections by gently rotating the pieces before finally fixing them. The two pieces should be held together firmly with crossed-over elastic bands or string going over the top of the scion and down underneath the pot. Some people use cocktail sticks or long cactus spines to hold the union together. This sounds more complicated than it is, but the illustrations will make it clearer.

Trichocereus is the best genus to use as a stock for larger plants. For tiny seedlings look for the slender stems of pereskia, which are more in proportion to the scion.

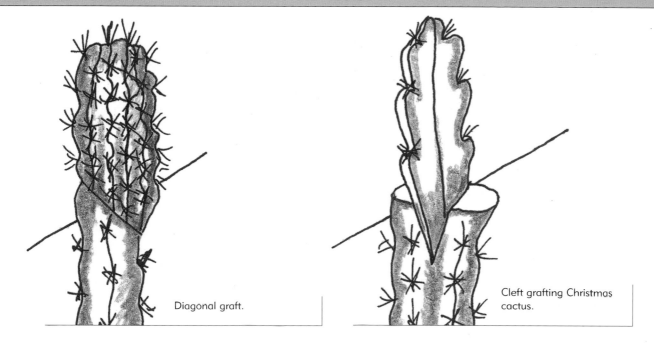

Diagonal graft.

Cleft grafting Christmas cactus.

The other method of grafting is to use a **cleft graft**. This is the method of choice for plants like Christmas cacti and epiphyllums, which have a softer structure and which will give very small cut surfaces. In this case the stock has a V-shaped cut made into it, and the flat scion is tapered to shape and pushed down into the cleft to a depth of about 25mm (1in). The stock and scion are held together with a long spine or a cocktail stick. Cleft grafts need a little longer to take than flat grafts: allow a week or so more and give them a

shadier position. The composite plant is then treated in exactly the same way as described for the flat graft method.

Do not water any of your grafted plants until you are certain that the graft has taken. Again, if in doubt, wait for a longer rather than shorter period every time.

Full to bursting: dense carpet planting such as these *Aloe brevifolia* would be prohibitively expensive without home propagation.

# CHAPTER 6
# LARGER PLANTS FOR ACCENT PLANTING

Size may not be everything, but there's no denying the dramatic impact of the taller-growing cacti – and the indoor climate you provide will be ideal for them

High point: the opuntias are popular 'accent' plants. *Opuntia subulata,* seen here, flowers only when it has grown very tall.

One of the advantages of growing plants indoors is that you are able to give them the conditions that most closely approximate those they would have in their native **habitat**, and this enables you to nurture large and showy specimens.

If you are planning to grow plants in a large bed in a conservatory, your plants will make the most rapid growth and will reach their maximum size in the shortest possible time. In many siutations, and certainly in the home, this is often impractical, so you will have to grow them in containers and regularly pot them on. If you don't do this you will in effect be practising a form of bonsai cultivation, since restricting the root run will slow down their growth – although this can, of course, be useful if space is limited.

Don't forget that you should be in control. Any plant which is getting too tall and which threatens to run out of headroom should be lopped without mercy. Not only will the mutilated plant sprout new heads, but you will also have a substantial cutting to root up. Some of the slender, more flexible, plants can be trained up the walls and then across, to create a rakish, prickly ceiling.

## TALL-GROWING TRUE CACTI

A number of cacti have a growth habit of forming tall columns, sometimes clumping into multiple stems and sometimes branching into what people think of as the traditional cowboy cactus. However, this species (*Carnegiea gigantea,* the giant saguaro cactus found in the southern USA), is so slow-growing that it takes 20 years in cultivation to reach 60cm (2ft) in height, and it is therefore strictly for the enthusiast. It is far better to substitute it with, say, *Opuntia subulata,* which, although basically columnar in form, will rapidly grow into an attractive spiny candelabrum shape if you decapitate it, and will rapidly reach 2m (6ft 6in) in height. Even better, if rapid growth is a priority, is to select one of the tall, cactus-like euphorbias mentioned under 'other succulents'.

Columnar cacti range from dark green-ribbed columns to those with pale, almost silver,

Hydra-headed: *Opuntia subulata* grows into a tall and impressive candelabrum if the top is removed.

stems covered with a variety of spines – from fine bristles to long, shaggy hair. Any species name with 'cereus' in it indicates that the plant has a columnar growing nature.

## CEPHALOCEREUS

*Cephalocereus chrysacanthus* is a tall-growing, branching plant producing slender columns with yellowish spines. In time, as the name suggests, the plant will develop a **cephalium**, which is a woolly or hairy hood at the top of the plant from which the large, pinkish-red flowers will appear.

*Cephalocereus dybowski* is a very attractive columnar species covered in soft white hair.

Bell-shaped white flowers will appear from a cephalium on older plants.

*Cephalocereus palmeri* is another columnar cactus, noticeably hairy even when young, with brown spines and a fluffy top, eventually forming a cephalium.

*Cephalocereus senilis*, one of the renowned old man cacti, is the only one sometimes known as the old man of the Andes. This is very showy, with masses of long and tangled white hair. It is, unfortunately, rather slow-growing, but since it seems to like a more restricted root run and a free-draining compost, it is well worth **underpotting**.

## CEREUS

*Cereus aethiops* is a worthwhile choice. It is a slender species reaching to almost 2m (5–6 ft). Its flowers, which are white, sometimes flushed pink, are produced at an earlier stage than most cereus.

*Cereus alacriportanus* has tall, bluish-green **cylindrical** stems up to 2m (6ft 6in) tall. Old specimens bear huge, 22cm (9in) long, very pale yellowish-pink flowers.

*Cereus chalybaeus* is a good find, with its attractive bluish columns, 5cm (2in) or more thick, bearing black spines on well-defined ribs.

*Cereus dayamii* has tall, pale green columns growing up to 25m (80ft) tall – eventually, and in its native habitat – and bearing massive 25cm (10in) long pure white flowers on old specimens. This species has few or no spines.

Serious cereus: huge white flowers will soon be opening on this *Cereus jamacaru*.

*Cereus forbesii* has blue-grey columns growing several metres high in the wild. As a result these are vigorous growers in cultivation and can be used for grafting more difficult species to speed up their growth. (See Chapter 5 on propagation.)

*Cereus grandicostatus* is an eye-catchingly azure blue when young, eventually becoming more yellowy-green. The tall columns produce huge 25cm (10in) white flowers.

*Cereus hankeanus* is a tall-growing, cylindrical plant which will rapidly give height to a collection, eventually reaching a few metres in height. It bears large white 12cm (5in) long flowers.

*Cereus jamacaru* has attractive bluish-green ribbed columns up to a metre (3ft) or so tall. It bears very large white flowers.

*Cereus peruvianus* produces tall-growing blue-green columns with six to eight ribs and large white flowers on old specimens.

*Cereus peruvianus × azureus* is a vigorous hybrid of two tall-growing blue-green stemmed columnar plants, so it is worth growing if you want quick **in-filling**. This species has huge white flowers.

*Cereus stenogonus* has branching, bluish-green columns with four or five ribs, and it grows up to 70cm (28in) tall. It will eventually produce large pink flowers. This is such a vigorous grower that it is an excellent candidate for grafting purposes.

*Cereus validus* is another quick-growing species, with bluish-green ribbed columns up to 2m (6ft) high and with large white to reddish flowers.

CLEISTOCACTUS

*Cleistocactus buchtienii* is a useful fast-growing, columnar cactus, forming clusters of tall stems with reddish-brown spines. It has wine red tubular flowers, 6cm (over 2in) long.

*Cleistocactus jujuyensis* forms beautiful cream-spined columns with long tubular flowers in an unusual bluish-carmine.

*Cleistocactus morawetzianus* has a shrubby or tree-like body with grey-green stems, pale spines and long white flowers with an odd, greenish or faintly pink sheen.

*Cleistocactus strausii* is a fabulous plant, with tall white columns covered in beautiful soft white spines. With time it will make slender and stately clumps. It has long scarlet flowers, rather disappointing in that they stay as almost rudimentary pink projections when you hope they will open into a huge starburst.

Reach for the sky: *Cleistocactus strausii* forms tall white columns – although there is also a much more humble cristate form, seen in the pot on the right of the picture next to a tall cereus.

Old boys' reunion: the shaggy white 'hair' of the oroecereus genus gives the plants their old man cacti nickname. This is *Oreocereus doelzianus*.

## OREOCEREUS

Also named borzicactus, these are known collectively as old man cacti because they have long, shaggy hair and, when grouped in a collection, suggest nothing so much as a gathering of the elderly in a rest home.

*Oreocereus celsianus* is tall-growing, over 1m (3ft), and covered in wispy white hair, with 9cm (almost 4in) long, dull pink flowers.

*Oreocereus doelzianus* grows up to 1m (3ft) tall, with **zygomorphic** (Christmas cactus-like) flowers, with a bluish-red colouring.

*Oreocereus celsianus* var. *fossulatus*, grows up to 2m tall (over 6ft), with long wispy white hairs and violet-red flowers.

## PERESKIA

These space-fillers make good conversation pieces because of their unlikely appearance.

*Pereskia aculeata* var. *godseffiana* is one of the most primitive and shrub-like of the

cacti, which has areoles with one to three spines but no **glochids.** It has very pretty peach-coloured leaves. Its eventual height is 2–3m (6-10ft), and its spread 1m (3ft).

*Pereskia grandifolia* is a very primitive form of true cactus, growing like a small shrub, and useful for a bushy effect. It is one of the earliest evolutionary stages in the development of the cacti we now see: very unusual. It has rose-like, purple flowers with pear-shaped fruits. It is good for the grafting of seedlings, as described on p.72. It will reach 5m (15ft), with a spread of 1m (3ft).

*Polaskia* (Stenocereus) *chichipe* forms pale green columns, branching from the base, and eventually growing up to 2m (over 6ft) tall. It has large creamy-white flowers.

Leader columns: the slender growths of *Polaskia chichipe* grow to more than 2m (more than 6ft).

## TRICHOCEREUS

Trichocereus (sometimes known as echinopsis) is a columnar-growing genus, large to tree-like, with large funnel-shaped flowers, often white, **diurnal** and scented, but occasionally coloured. The ones originating from Chile have flowers which stay open for several days. They are good grafting-stock plants, and the easiest of all cacti to root from cuttings and offsets.

*Trichocereus candicans* is a branching, tall-growing 'cowboy'-type cactus, bearing large, 20 cm (8in) long, strongly perfumed, white flowers.

*Trichocereus litoralis* has white flowers 14cm (almost 6in) long by 10cm (4in) in diameter which, unusually, stay open for up to five days. Erect and columnar, it can arch under its own weight, new growth from this becoming vertical again.

*Trichocereus spachiana* forms tall, dark green columns which are freely branching. It has very impressive blooms, which grow up to 20cm (8in) long by 15cm (6in) wide, with white inner petals and greenish tinged outer petals.

*Trichocereus valida* is a stout and erect columnar, fast-growing plant with large white flowers.

## OPUNTIA

The opuntia genus is excellent for creating a large presence in your cactus bed or conservatory planters, and for providing dramatic accent plants in the house. The

TOP: Trichocereus species in flower.
CENTRE: *Trichocereus candicans*.
BOTTOM: *Opuntia basilaris*.

Stealing the show: *Opuntia leucotricha*, like other plants in this genus, is a great attention-grabber.

plants come in a surprising variety of size and shape. There are taller-growing species available as slender columns, while tree- and shrub-like species grow by producing a succession of round and oval pads, as in the classical prickly pear varieties.

*Opuntia acanthocarpa* has branching cylindrical stems up to 2m (over 6ft) high, with large red and yellow flowers.

*Opuntia basilaris* is a very attractive species with grey-blue pads, fine spines and brown glochids. The pads are often heart-shaped.

*Opuntia bergeriana* has spiny, bright green pads, 10–25cm (4–10in) long by 5–10 cm (2–4in) wide, clustering freely, and it can eventually reach 2–3m (6–9ft or so) in height. It has readily produced red flowers.

*Opuntia chlorotica* has large bluish-green stems on a branching stem which grows up to 2m (over 6ft) tall.

*Opuntia cylindrica* is a useful, tall-growing cylindrical plant with large yellow flowers.

*Opuntia imbricata* has strongly spined, tall, branching, cylindrical stems up to 3m (9ft) tall, with purple and yellow flowers.

*Opuntia leucotricha* has large velvety pads, 20cm (8in) long, with bristly spines. It eventually develops a trunk and can reach several metres high.

*Opuntia lindheimeri* var. *linguiformis* is a bushy plant growing up to 1m (3ft). Its large oval pads have only a few spines. It bears large flowers which are predominantly yellow, fading to red.

*Opuntia phaeacantha* is a bushy plant with oval pads and yellow flowers.

*Opuntia spinosior* eventually grows into a tree-like plant with large yellow or purple flowers.

*Opuntia subulata* is similar to *opuntia cylindrica*. It has rapidly growing clustering columns, and it can be made to branch dramatically if you cut it back regularly. It can be trained to arch overhead like a weird, prickly arbour. Eventually it has red flowers, but it does need to be very large before it will bloom.

*Opuntia violacea* has really pretty lilac-tinged grey pads, which are large and oval. It reaches up to about 2m (over 6ft) tall and it carries attractive large yellow flowers with a red throat.

Music hall joke: *Echinocactus grusonii* has an unflattering popular name.

Architectural: as its name suggests, *Euphorbia candelabrum* var. *erythrae* is a many-branched plant.

*Opuntia violacea* var. *macrocentra* grows up to 1m (3ft) tall with bluish-green pads about 12cm (5in) wide. It has yellow flowers.

For a complete contrast, take a look at:

*Echinocactus grusonii*, the golden barrel cactus or, less kindly, mother-in-law's chair or cushion. These are fat, globular cacti, covered in stout yellow spines, becoming very large with age, like big fat pumpkins. There is also a white-spined form.

## COLUMNAR-GROWING OTHER SUCCULENTS

Euphorbia is a massive genus, which includes many traditional garden shrubs. However, some of the euphorbias can grow into magnificent tall-branched specimens, which are remarkably cactus-like in appearance and will grow into 2m (6ft 6in) specimens much more quickly than the true cacti.

These euphorbia species are interesting plants in that they have developed along parallel evolutionary lines to the cacti, with the same strategies for conserving moisture, but the cacti have developed in the New World of the Americas, whereas euphorbias have developed on the African continent.

There are, in consequence, some interesting differences. The euphorbias, for instance, have clung on to vestigial leaves. Often a deep, glossy green, they grow much more quickly. This is an advantage if you are in a hurry to fill a space, but it also means that they have a tendency to outgrow their homes, so you need to balance these features.

All euphorbias have a milky, irritant sap, so take care to handle them with gloves if they are damaged in any way and oozing.

*Euphorbia candelabrum* var. *erythraea* has dark green stems with a lighter green central band. It forms branches like a candelabrum with small leaves, and is very architectural.

*Euphorbia canariensis* has stout, branching columns, four- or five- angled, with flat sides between. It is eventually very tall, and can reach several metres in height.

*Euphorbia coerulescens* is a blue-grey branched shrub, reaching 1.5m (5ft), with 1.5cm (½in) long spines and a yellow **inflorescence**. See the large picture on page 74.

*Euphorbia enopla* has branching, thorny six- or seven- angled stems, growing up to 1m (3ft) high. It carries small yellow flowers

*Euphorbia mauritanica* is the milk tree of the Boers – but please don't drink it! The common name refers to the extremely irritant milky sap it exudes when damaged. It is a thornless shrub, which branches from the base and grows up to 1.5m (5ft) tall.

*Euphorbia resinifera* is a very thick-stemmed species, soon forming giant clumps. It displays yellow flowers.

Taking over: *Euphorbia resinifera* grows in large and thick-stemmed clumps.

Black beauty: *Aeonium arboreum* 'Zwartkop' turns very dark when exposed to strong sunlight.

*Aeonium arboreum* 'Atropurpureum' has very attractive deep maroon rosettes, contrasting well with the type species.

*Aeonium arboreum* 'Variegatum' is another useful plant, with contrasting foliage.

*Aeonium arboreum* 'Zwartkop' is a really useful cultivar, which is far darker than *A. arboreum* 'Atropurpureum' and very impressive, with glossy-black rosettes on long stems. Again, this goes well in a mixed planting, to contrast with lime green *A. arboreum*. Both of the purple aeoniums will colour up more strongly if they are given a spell outside in the summer. This also strengthens the stems, which otherwise have a disturbing habit of dropping off when knocked. It's true that you will get more plants if you root the broken pieces like cuttings, but this can be annoying.

*Aeonium undulatum*. This attractive species has silver-grey stems to 1m (3ft) tall, with large, glossy dark green rosettes and dark yellow flowers.

*Cotyledon wallichii* has thick, branching stems covered with the stumps of old leaves. It has attractive, peeling bark, and grey-green, long, narrow, succulent leaves and yellow flowers. It grows up to 2m (over 6ft) tall, but it is slow-growing.

*Crassula ovata*, or the money plant, is confusingly also known as *C. argentea* and *C. portulacea*, and it will be found under all three names. The species and its cultivars make wonderful mass plantings in a bed or large container, where the foliage contrast looks very fine. The true species is said to have good *feng shui*, guaranteeing prosperity,

## OTHER LARGE SUCCULENTS

Look for the Canary Island aeoniums, which make fabulous tall plants which are showy and architectural.

*Aeonium arboreum* has smooth, branching stems bearing bright green rosettes. It grows up to 1m (3ft) tall, and it can be encouraged to branch into a substantial bushy shrub by taking pieces off the top. This also gives you cuttings (see Chapter 3). It has golden-yellow flowers.

Sundowner: *Crassula ovata* 'Hummel's Sunset' has striking yellow, red and green leaves.

Blushing: *Crassula ovata* 'Pink Beauty'.

which is why you see it in Chinese restaurants. It has a thick trunk and many branches, with glossy, coin-shaped leaves and small white flowers in the winter. It can reach 2m (over 6ft) in height.

*Crassula ovata* 'Blue Bird' is a pretty cultivar which has grey-green leaves.

*Crassula ovata* 'Hummel's Sunset' is a very colourful cultivar, with heavily variegated yellow, red and green leaves, especially when grown in strong light.

*Yucca elephantipes* is a common houseplant, but as it belongs to the Agavaceae it sneaks in here as a really useful, quick-growing succulent. Most yuccas are fully hardy, and even this one will survive in milder areas in the garden. In the conservatory it will soon grow into a significant-sized shrub or small tree, making an exotic and architectural impact, with distinctive multiple trunks forming near the ground. It has long, narrow, pointed leaves, which are rather leathery, and larger plants will produce attractive **panicles** of pendant, tulip-shaped flowers in the summer.

*Yucca elephantipes* 'Variegata' is a useful, more colourful cultivar, striped with white margins to the edges of the leaves.

## ROSETTES

### AGAVES

Agaves are wonderful, spiky architectural plants, with sword-like leaves growing in rosettes. They include very choice variegated varieties, as well as having leaves from the longest, thinnest needle-like spikes to great squat, fat short ones. They make dramatic focal points in large containers, grow impressively if they are given an unrestricted root run in conservatory beds and also make a huge architectural impact in a large container indoors. They will thrive in all conditions, even in an unheated conservatory over the winter if they are kept dry. They have to be huge to flower, but since this will kill the parent plant it is a marvel best not experienced.

Prickly character: *Agave americana*, like others of the genus, has wickedly sharp terminal spines.

Handle them with care, because the thick, leathery leaves often have sharp-toothed edges and ferocious **terminal spines.** Plant them well out of reach of children and pets, and don't put them at eye level. It's a good idea, anyway, to remove the terminal spines with scissors or secateurs if they are anywhere near through-routes, or close to where you might sit or stand.

## LARGE SPECIES FOR HIGH-IMPACT PLANTING SCHEMES:

*Agave colorata* grows into rosettes up to 1m (3ft) across with broad, tapering leaves which are an attractive ash-grey with pink bands.

*Agave americana* has stiff, tooth-edged, blue-green leaves forming a rosette.

*Agave americana* 'Mediopicta' and *Agave americana* 'Mediopicta Alba' are rare and desirable, with a strong yellow or white mid-stripe on the dark green leaves.

*Agave americana* 'Variegata' grows into a huge rosette, 2m (6ft) or more across with long, tapering leaves which have broad cream-yellow edges.

Distinctly weird: the wavy branches of *Alluaudia procera* can reach up to 15m (45ft) in the plant's native habitat.

*Agave palmeri* has narrow grey-green leaves forming large rosettes.

*Agave palmeri* var. *chrysantha* forms a handsome rosette of long curving leaves.

*Agave mckelveyana* has rosettes of grey-green narrow tapering leaves up to 1m (3ft) across.

*Agave utahensis* subsp. *kaibabensis* forms light green rosettes up to 1m (3ft) across, with long, tapering leaves.

*Agave univittata* makes offsetting rosettes with glossy green leaves up to 1m (3ft) long, with darker longitudinal stripes. It has toothed leaf edges.

*Alluaudia procera* is a large-growing plant, reaching 15m (50ft or so) in habitat, but not in your house or conservatory, of course. Its few weird, almost sinuous, branches with thorny edges and small, oval-shaped leaves, make it a distinctive architectural choice. It has small yellowish-green flowers.

*Agave americana* 'Variegata'.

Looks familiar: aloe flowers are reminiscent of red hot pokers.

## ALOES

Another high-impact genus, which will soon give mass to your planting ideas. The species described below have leaves arranged in a rosette form. The leaves can be triangular or long and thin, sometimes striped or spotted. In habitat they can reach 20 metres in height. Their flowers are yellow, orange or red, and they grow on long, arching stalks. At a glance the flowers bear a resemblance to those of red hot pokers.

*Aloe arborescens* has a stout, tall-growing stem up to 2m (over 6ft) high, with dark green fleshy rosettes of strongly toothed tapering leaves. It has tubular red flowers on a long stem.

*Aloe broomii* has bright green rosettes of broad, tapering leaves with spiky edges, up to 1m (3ft) in diameter. It produces greenish-yellow flowers on a long stalk.

*Aloe dichotoma* is an attractive branching shrub with rosettes of long, thin blue-green leaves. With age, it grows to a few metres tall. It has yellow flowers.

*Aloe gariepensis* has branching stems to 1m (3ft) high, and dark green leaves with white spots and horny edges. It produces a tall inflorescence with yellow flowers.

*Aloe marlothii* has greenish-blue, spiny, tapering leaves forming a rosette and orange flowers. It will eventually grow to 1m (3ft) tall, and sometimes a little more.

*Aloe plicatilis* is one of the most distinctive of the tree aloes, with forked stems which can reach 5m (16ft) in height. It has fan-like clusters of strap-shaped leaves, grey-green, which are 30cm (12in) long and 4cm (1½in) wide, arranged in opposite rows. This plant bears red flowers.

*Aloe vera* has long, tapering leaves, usually spotted white. It forms dense groups and can grow up to 2m (6ft 6in) or so. It has yellow flowers. It is thought to have all sorts of medicinal and cosmetic properties, and is a familiar ingredient of shampoos and skin creams. For all that, it has to be said, it is not one of the best-looking aloes.

Forked tongues: *Aloe plicatilis* is a distinctive plant with spreading strap-shaped leaves.

# CHAPTER 7
# LOWER-GROWING PLANTS

The taller, showier specimens would lose
their effect without the massed flowers
and foliage that cluster at their feet

Although this category may sound dull, it is actually very important to have plenty of these plants to make sure that you have a massed effect, avoiding the glass-covered equivalent of the beginner gardener's downfall – those lonely rows of single tulips flowering about a foot apart, or herbaceous borders with more soil than plants. Wherever you are planning to grow them (unless, of course, you are going for individual spotlit 'stars') they will make an important contribution to your display. These are the plants which go in front of the climbers, trailers and large accent plants and behind the smaller plants chosen for flower or form, such as living stones and caudiciforms.

Luckily cacti and other succulents are very good for producing upright, medium-sized and small filler planting. These lower-growing plants act as a backdrop for some of your flashier choices and also make an impact in their own right. The cacti offer a variety of architectural shapes for **infilling** because of their spination, and they come in a range of shades from brightest green to whites, greys and yellows. Succulents offer you a huge colour range, with every shade of green, plus variegated plants in green plus white, cream,

yellow and even pink and red. There are also self-colours in just about every shade from palest grey and lilac through crimson and maroon to deepest purple-black. You have the choice, therefore, of selecting plants on purely aesthetic grounds. You could colour-theme your planting and try combinations of sophisticated greys, lilacs and purples, or go for a really 'hot' look, with bright yellows, limes and glossy greens.

For an instant effect, you will need to use the other succulents in the main, because these have a bushier, leafier habit and will make rapid growth. Genera to consider include the aloes, with their tapering leaves, and the incredibly diverse shapes and forms of the crassulas. Euphorbias are relatively fast growing and as well as being useful for giving you large specimens, as in Chapter 6, they also come in a variety of cactus-like shapes, as well as shrubby and globular forms which resemble nothing else in the plant kingdom. The echeverias are also a must-have. Their colourful rosettes offer every colour you could hope for, from palest pinks through

Curly top: echeverias, such as this 'Mauna Loa', are wonderful foliage plants.

Cover-up: echeverias are among a large choice of low-growing plants which can be used to cover otherwise bare areas of soil.

turquoise and blue to virtually black, and they range in size from coffee cup to dinner plate.

Of course, there is a place for cactus specimens, too, but these are a longer term proposition, while the other succulents will grow quickly and soon give structure to your planting. True cacti do make a really strong impact, however, especially if you go for plants with ferocious spines like bristling hedgehogs, or those with spines resembling long fish hooks, chosen from the ferocacti and mammillarias.

## TRUE CACTI

### OPUNTIA
The Opuntias are an exception to the leisurely habit of growth amongst the cacti. This makes them a hugely useful genus – which also, of course, provides rapidly growing tall specimens, as discussed in Chapter 6.

There are also many shrubby, **prostrate** and creeping forms, however, as well as some stockier upright growers. Although they do flower quite readily, these plants are especially useful for their structure and form.

### Prostrate forms
*Opuntia chaffeyi* is prostrate and freely branching, with long thin stems issuing from a large, fleshy root. The flowers are lemon yellow.

*Opuntia compressa* is a prostrate plant, forming creeping and spreading clumps of dark green, oval pads up to 10cm (4in) across, and it is easier to handle than some opuntias because there are few, if any, spines. It produces large yellow flowers. Because they will grow outside they will make rapid growth with the additional heat they enjoy in a conservatory or indoors.

*Opuntia erectoclada* grows with small creeping pads and soon forms a colony. It offers a contrast with its glossy, deep carmine-red flowers.

*Opuntia macrohiza* grows prostrate, in colonies. It has large bluish-green segments with few or no spines, and large yellow flowers with a red centre.

*Opuntia pestifer* has prostrate, elongated segmented stems and light yellow flowers.

*Opuntia polyacantha* is another bushy, prostrate plant with spiny pads and yellow flowers.

*Opuntia retrorsa* is a creeping species, forming groups of long thin segments and producing yellow flowers.

*Opuntia taylorii* has long cylindrical segments forming a prostrate shrub with yellow flowers.

*Opuntia tortispina* is a scrambling plant with circular or oval pads, white, often twisted, spines and sulphur yellow flowers.

*Opuntia tortispina* var. *cymochila* is another prostrate scrambler made up of circular pads about 8cm (3in) across. It has very large yellow flowers.

## Upright forms

*Opuntia brasilensis* has fresh green miniature pads and yellow flowers.

*Opuntia elata* is another, easier to handle, opuntia, which has smooth, rounded, dark glossy-green pads with very few, if any, spines and orange-red flowers.

*Opuntia hystricina* is a low-growing, clump-forming species with almost circular pads, often flushed pink or purple, and large yellow flowers.

*Opuntia microdasys* is one you will recognize, with its beautiful flat pads displaying tufts of cream hairs or, in variety, very yellow hairs. This is the renowned bunnies' ears. It isn't as friendly as it sounds, though, as the tiny spines are incredibly irritating if they get into your fingers.

*Opuntia microdasys* var. *albispina*, with elegant white tufts of hairs on flat, pale green pads. These hairs are soft to the touch and rarely detach themselves into fingers.

*Opuntia microdasys* var. *rufida* f. *minima* is a real gem – a small and very compact padded variety.

*Opuntia monacatha variegata* has pale green flattened stems, very attractively marbled with cream and yellow.

*Opuntia rufida* has flat pads with attractive red brown areoles.

*Opuntia stenopetala* has greyish-green pads, and its orange-red flowers are easily produced on quite small specimens. It is a fast-growing species.

*Opuntia tuna* is a shrubby, branching plant with bright green pads. Its large yellow and red flowers are readily produced.

*Opuntia verschaffeltii* is another cylindrical species and one of the easier opuntias to flower, producing red blooms quite readily.

*Opuntia vestita* is an attractive, pale cylindrical plant, covered with fluffy white hair. Excellent for contrasts.

## FEROCACTUS

Ferocactus is a heavily spined genus, with a distinctive, large, fat globular form which has given its members the common name of barrel cacti.

*Ferocactus glaucescens* is a bluish-green spherical plant which produces yellow flowers when quite young – an unusual feature for a ferocactus.

*Opuntia rufida.*

Ferocactus.

Ferocactus peninsulae.

*Ferocactus hamatacanthus* has long, slender white spines and yellow flowers with red throats.

*Ferocactus peninsulae* is a very heavily spined barrel cactus.

*Ferocactus peninsulae* var. *townsendianus* has a shortly cylindrical-shaped body with attractive ribs, often spiralled or wavy. The flowers are pink in the middle with a greenish-yellow border.

## MAMMILLARIA

Some of the mammillaria species are really good plants for interesting and attractive spines, rather than, or as well as, for their flowers (see Chapter 9). The following rank among the best of them:

*Mammillaria albicans* is a cylindrical plant up to 20cm (8in) high covered in showy, pure white spines. It has large white flowers with a pale pink **mid-stripe**.

*Mammillaria albicoma* is a small-growing, clustering species, covered in thick white wool and with greenish-white flowers.

*Mammillaria albilanata* var. *reppenhagenii* is a beautiful tight white-spined plant from the elegans group.

*Mammillaria angelensis* has fabulous white spines and large, bell-shaped white flowers.

*Mammillaria bocasana* is a clustering cream-flowered species with masses of white wool and white spines.

*Mammillaria bombycina* has very attractive spines, and soon makes imposing clumps.

*Mammillaria celsiana* (syn *M. muehlenpfordtii*) is a nice-looking yellow-spined plant with deep pink flowers.

*Mammillaria decipiens* var. *camptotricha* is also known as the bird's nest cactus. It has very long, showy, curved and interlacing soft spines and white flowers.

Mammillaria bocasana.

*Mammillaria bombycina.*

*Mammillaria duwei* is a very desirable small clumping plant, with attractive white hair and spines.

*Mammillaria elongata* is a columnar plant with golden yellow spines and cream flowers. It has the advantage of rapidly clustering.

*Mammillaria hahniana* is a desirable species with long white hairs and purple flowers.

*Mammillaria lanata* (also known as *M. supertexta*) is a lovely plant covered in short white spines. It has small reddish flowers, immersed in a mass of long white wool.

*Mammillaria lenta* is a magnificent tight white-spined species, with white flowers, and is known as the snowball cactus.

*Mammillaria microthele* has attractive white bristly spines.

*Mammillaria parkinsonii* is another good variety, noteworthy for its covering of strong white spines.

*Mammillaria pennispinosa* is a delightful species, immediately recognizable by its beautiful white, feathery spines.

*Mammillaria prolifera* develops into fluffy cream mounds, rapidly clustering.

*Mammillaria senilis* is one of the most beautiful of all cacti. The fluffy white plants are completely covered in silvery white spines, and mature plants cluster. It also has large red flowers.

*Mammillaria spinosissima* 'Pico' is an attractive cultivar with very long, fine white spines and deep pink flowers.

ALOE
These have been mentioned as large plants for architectural placement. There are, however, smaller-growing rosette-shaped aloes which, with their long, fleshy leaves resembling weird starfish, are useful structural plants. They grow rapidly enough to make them strong contenders.

*Aloe aristata* is a narrow-leaved rosette, with a very tall flower stalk and orange-red flowers.

*Aloe brevifolia* produces clustering rosettes of thick grey leaves, with red flowers.

*Aloe buhrii* is a stemless, rosette-forming aloe which forms multi-headed clumps with age. It is low growing, with leaves which are 40cm (16in) long and 9cm (3½in) across at the base. The leaves are yellow to grey-green with oblong or H-shaped pale markings and reddish margins. The leaf edges are smooth or slightly toothed. It has orange-red, occasionally yellow, flowers.

*Aloe ciliaris* is an unusual, rambling aloe, which makes long masses of triangular green rosettes. It can also be encouraged to climb up a trellis.

*Aloe davyana* has rosettes of thick, tapering leaves with bands of white spots. It has unusual, pink flowers on a long stalk.

*Aloe ferox*, the bitter aloe, has fiercely spined, grey, succulent leaves and red flowers on a tall spike.

*Aloe grandidentata* is good for coverage, as it produces numerous suckers to form large, dense groups of bright green rosettes spotted white. It has orange flowers.

*Aloe humilis* has 10cm (4in) long, waxy, grey-green leaves which are inward curving, and red flowers.

*Aloe microstigma* has long narrow leaves, speckled with white and with reddish teeth along the edges. It has red buds, turning into yellow flowers.

*Aloe mitriformis* is another creeping aloe, with sprawling stems and thick fleshy blue-green leaves with small, toothed edges.

*Aloe pretoriensis* is one of the most beautiful aloes, forming neat rosettes of bluish-green leaves and producing bright red flowers.

*Aloe saponaria* is a generally stemless aloe, forming flat, open rosettes although with age it may produce a short stem, less than 1m (3ft) tall. It has broad and variable leaves, very spotted, light green and 15–20cm (6–8in) long, triangular, with dried twisted ends and sharp, brown marginal teeth. Its flowers can be red, orange or yellow.

*Aloe striata* has stemless rosettes, leaves 40–50cm (16–20in) long with white marginal teeth and coral red flowers.

*Aloe variegata*, is the partridge-breasted aloe. This has thick green, triangular leaves, variegated with white. It carries red flowers on a long stem.

Left to right: *Aloe buhrii, Aloe davyana, Aloe ciliaris.*

## AEONIUM

The first three of these aeoniums are particularly useful, because they make a really colourful foliage display which acts as a pretty and effective medium-sized space filler. They look well planted together, with some plain, dark green foliage plants to act as a foil.

*Aeonium domesticum* 'Variegatum' is a colourful, green and yellow, compact miniature shrub.

*Aeonium haworthia* 'Variegatum' is an attractive, branching bush to 60cm (24in) high, which has thin stems bearing rosettes of yellow, red and green leaves. It produces white flowers.

*Aeonium holochrysum* is a freely branching shrub with large, 20cm (8in) diameter rosettes of yellowish-green leaves with a showy red mid-stripe and red margins. It has many small yellow flowers displayed on a tall spike.

*Aeonium tabuliforme* produces bright green, flat rosettes growing to the size of a dinner plate.

*Aeonium virgineum* is mat-forming, with green leaves tinged red in the sun, and an elongating stem.

*Aeonium virgineum.*

## AGAVE

Agaves, mentioned in the previous chapter, also produce smaller-growing and very choice species, with the same rosette shape. They are good specimen houseplants, as well as making a strong impact in conservatory beds.

*Agave bracteosa* forms pale green rosettes of curved, narrow leaves, 35–50cm long (14–20in). It has no terminal spine.

*Agave ferdinandi-regis* makes attractive rosettes of triangular leaves edged white.

*Agave filifera*, the thread agave, is very attractive, with long, tapering, rigid leaves, which are glossy green, with white lines and long fibres splitting from the edges.

*Agave lechuguilla* has rosettes which grow up to 75cm (30in) across, with numerous offsets. The leaves are blue-green and sickle-shaped, growing to about 30cm (12in) long with brown teeth along the edges and a long 2cm (almost 1in) brown spine at the end. The upper surfaces of the leaves have faint stripes, the undersides closely spaced lines.

*Agave parrasana* has chubby looking 60cm (24in) rosettes, blue-grey. The leaves, which are up to 30cm (12in) long and 10–15cm (4–6in) wide, are edged with black teeth and a black terminal spine.

*Agave parryi* forms compact rosettes up to 80cm (32in) in diameter. It has long, tapering leaves with a grey bloom. As it is **hardy** outside in the UK, it will make rapid growth for you in the conservatory or the house.

*Agave shawii* has mat-forming rosettes of long, tapering glossy green leaves with horny margins.

Left: *Agave parrasana*.
Above: *Agave victoriae-reginae*.

*Agave toumeyana* has narrow pointed leaves with white markings and fine threads on the edges. It forms a rosette which spreads up to 50cm (20in) across.

*Agave utahensis* has grey-green tapering leaves forming rosettes which grow up to 70cm (28in) across.

*Agave victoriae-reginae* is a fabulous plant, with stiff, pointed succulent leaves forming a rosette. Its dark green leaves edged with white are so tightly interlinked, and the colours are so contrasting, that the plant almost looks artificial.

CRASSULA
This useful genus offers an unbeatable range of species, which are almost infinitely variable. As a result, they appear in one guise or another in every chapter of this book. They are trouble-free plants, which grow vigorously, and will tolerate any position from sunny to shaded, with consequent alterations to the size and colour of their foliage. They are very easy to propagate from cuttings.

These species are attractive and varied plants, grown for their colourful foliage effects, interesting forms and leaf shapes:

*Crassula anomala* grows into a small shrub with tiny, pointed, red-tinged leaves and a profusion of small white flowers.

*Crassula arta* has dense columns of crowded, thick, keel-shaped leaves covered in an attractive a pale grey bloom. It carries clusters of small white flowers.

*Crassula alba* is a rosette-forming plant, which has pointed, fleshy leaves with finely serrated edges and white flowers.

*Crassula columnella* grows, as the name suggests, in strange, compressed columns of green to yellow-green leaves which develop a red tint in strong sunlight. It reaches 15cm (6in) in height, with stems which are 8–10cm (3–4in) tall, and it bears greenish-white flowers.

*Crassula anomala* in flower.

*Crassula falcata* is worth growing for its spirals of blue-grey **bloomed**, succulent leaves, as well as for its masses of red flowers.

*Crassula humilis* grows into a low shrubby plant with thick grey-green keel-shaped leaves, usually tinged red. It has clusters of small white flowers.

*Crassula lactea* is a bushy species, growing up to 40cm (16in) high with large thick leaves and lots of white flowers in winter.

*Crassula mesembryanthemopsis* has thick, whitish-grey, truncated triangular leaves, and it grows in an interesting mound shape. The flowers are white.

*Crassula muscosa* has thin stems a few centimetres tall, and these are covered in minute green leaves.

*Crassula obliqua* 'Variegata' has very showy grass green leaves, strongly marked with lemon and cream.

*Crassula obliqua* var. *gollum*, is an unusual plant, with the leaves folded and united into solid tapering cylinders. A must!

*Crassula sarcocaulis* make compact shrubs, attractively tree-like, with dark trunks and tiny leaves. It has pink flowers in autumn. It is hardy outside, so will thrive in a cold conservatory, although it will also tolerate the warmer conditions indoors.

*Crassula sarcocaulis* subsp. *rupicola* has white flowers.

*Crassula tecta* has small, thick, grey-spotted leaves which form tight clusters. The flowers are white.

*Crassula tomentosa.* The plant grows up to 60cm (24in) tall. It has densely hairy, grey-green leaves arranged in loose rosettes and small, pale yellow flowers.

*Dudleya antonyi* has rosettes of long tapering leaves with an interesting chalky white or grey surface. It grows up to 50cm (20in) in diameter and has numerous red flowers borne on a tall stem.

*Dudleya farinosa* is similar, with pale, chalky rosettes.

KALANCHOE
Kalanchoes also appear in many shapes and sizes, including the following useful shrubs with attractive foliage colour:

*Kalanchoe daigremontiana*, or mother of thousands, has tall stems with triangular grey-olive leaves which develop miniature

*Dudleya antonyi.*

*Portulacaria afra.*

replica plants from their edges. These drop off and form little colonies. Children love them.

*Kalanchoe fedtschenkoi* grows into a small bush with blue-green leaves with brown margins, and brownish-pink flowers.

*Kalanchoe fedtschenkoi* 'Variegata' is a really colourful species, which has beautiful blue-grey leaves with yellow and cream markings edged with red.

*Kalanchoe pubescens* is a robust, tall-growing plant with thick, hairy, triangular-shaped chunky leaves.

*Kalanchoe tomentosa* is a much sought-after beauty with grey, furry leaves patterned with brown and yellow markings.

PACHYPHYTUM
These make a good, pale, contrast with other plants, their grey-lilac leaves being covered in a soft bloom.

*Pachyphytum compactum* forms tight clumps of grey-green succulent leaves.

*Pachyphytum glutinicaule* has thick, rounded leaves covered with a fine grey bloom, and light red flowers.

*Pachyphytum hookeri* has oval leaves covered in a pink-grey bloom. The flowers are red.

*Portulacaria afra*, with its red stems and angular branches, rapidly makes a small shrub. It is especially useful in its variegated form, with green and yellow leaves, *P. afra* 'Foliisvariegatus'.

*Puya chilensis* is a short, woody-stemmed shrub crowned by a dense rosette of long, tapering, arching leaves. It has tubular, metallic yellow flowers growing from a much-branched stem. Be warned, however, that this is one of the most hostile plants to handle, with stiff, lacerating spines which seem to show real malice. Handle with the folded newspaper trick illustrated on p. 55.

*Senecio haworthii.*

*Senecio articulatus* is known as the candle plant, because of its pale, finger-thick, jointed stems, which are grey or green with red or brown markings. The plant grows up to 70cm (28in) high, and it will develop heads of delicate leaves if it is given sufficient water. It has yellow flowers.

*Senecio haworthii* reaches 30cm (12in) high, with silvery grey-green 5cm (2in) long leaves which grow in spirals, and orange or yellow flowers.

ECHEVERIA

These are some of the best foliage plants you can possibly have. Many beautiful cultivars have been developed, and their rosettes come in a range of pastel shades, pinks, turquoises and lilacs, through really dark maroons to almost black. Planted up together they make fabulous contrasting arrangements. They can also be used to set off taller accent plants if used as a colourful underplanting in a container, and they are really pretty planted up *en masse* in a container full of a single cultivar.

*Echeveria affinis* has impressive dark olive green rosettes, almost black.

*Echeveria* 'Afterglow' has impressive large, deep red-to-purple rosettes.

*Echeveria albicans* has powdery grey-blue leaves, forming an attractive rosette.

*Echeveria* 'Blue Curls' has a rosette of wavy blue-green leaves.

*Echeveria* 'Black Prince', like all the dark echeverias, is highly prized. It has red-maroon to almost black leaves.

*Echeveria carnicolor* forms clumps of pink-lilac leaves.

*Echeveria derenbergii* is a tight, grey-bloomed, compact rosette.

*Echeveria dereceana* has beautiful rosettes of pointed grey or grey-brown leaves.

*Echeveria elegans* is a branching species with an intense grey bloom.

*Echeveria* 'Easter Bonnet' has really attractive rosettes of grey, blue-green leaves with crinkled edges.

*Echeveria glauca* has grey-bloomed leaves in large, clustering, rosettes.

*Echeveria* 'Harry Butterfield' has dramatically coloured round green leaves with bright red edges. The leaf edges are slightly wavy, the rosettes medium-sized.

*Echeveria* 'Perle von Nurnberg'.

*Echeveria* 'Harry Butterfield'.

*Echeveria* 'Easter Bonnet'.

*Echeveria lindsayana* has striking rosettes of pointed blue-grey leaves, tipped with red.

*Echeveria* 'Mauna Loa' (named after a Hawaiian volcano) is multi-coloured bronze and olive green. See page 90 for picture.

*Echeveria meridian* has vigorous, bright green rosettes which reach 30cm (12in) across.

*Echeveria nodulosa* 'Painted Beauty' is a striking cultivar. Its green leaves have strongly contrasting red and brown streaks and patches all over them.

*Echeveria* 'Painted Frills' has rosettes of wavy red, brown and olive-green leaves.

*Echeveria peacockii* has rosettes of long tapering blue-white leaves.

*Echeveria* 'Perle von Nurnberg' is an amazing pale lilac cultivar.

*Echeveria* 'Rondellii' has blue-green rosettes of tapering, bristly leaves.

*Echeveria* 'Red Edge' develops large rosettes of rounded to slightly wavy leaves. Green, and marked with red lines and patches, these have bright red edges. The flower spike is very stout.

*Echeveria runyonii* 'Topsy-turvy' offsets freely to form clumps of long grey leaves, widening at the tips and with the leaf sides curling inwards.

*Echeveria setosa* is a very unusual plant and one of the best echeverias, with attractive green-grey leaves covered with dense white hairs.

*Echeveria subrigida* has large, very pretty grey-blue rosettes which reach up to 60cm (2ft) across.

*Echeveria subsessilis* has rosettes of blue-grey leaves with red edges.

SOME SIMILAR PLANTS

*Graptopetalum pentandrum* subsp. *superbum* has succulent leaves with a distinctive purplish-grey bloom.

*Graptoveria* 'Hahinii' has elongated rosettes of grey leaves flushed pink.

*Graptoveria* 'Opalina' has thick, oval leaves covered in a red-grey bloom and arranged in a rosette.

*Pacheveria scheideckeri* 'Chimera' has attractive blue-grey rosettes.

*Hoya multiflora* is, unlike the climbing or trailing species in Chapter 8, a shrub-like upright hoya which is very free-flowering. Its drawn-back flower lobes give it a shooting star appearance.

*Sedum pachyphyllum* is low-growing and shrubby, reaching 25cm (10in) with fat, oval green leaves which appear very red-edged in good light.

*Echeveria glauca.*

*Echeveria elegans.*

*Graptoveria* 'Hahinii'.

# CHAPTER 8
# TRAILING AND CLIMBING PLANTS

Nothing looks better than a selection of climbing and
trailing plants, giving an impression of lushness
and fecundity impossible to achieve in any other way

Spilling over: a cascade pot of winter flowering crassulas.

Thirstier trailing plants generally make a lot of work in the house because they need daily watering, and this makes them difficult to use on any scale, but the cacti and other succulents need so little watering that you can use them as hanging plants much more lavishly in the home or in the elaborate conservatory.

In the house you can suspend hanging containers with built-in drip trays, or hanging cachepots, into which you can place pots of lush hanging foliage. These can frame your windows and soften the edges of shelves and tables. You can use them in planted containers, twining them around a variety of supports, from bamboo canes to elaborate tiny obelisks. Cascade pots can make foliage waterfalls as feature plants on tables, in niches and on plinths.

Succulent plants are also a good choice in a bathroom, where you can hang a jungle of trailing plants which will need hardly any attention because they will absorb water from the steam. They can also fill those really high windows which are too difficult to reach for daily watering.

In the conservatory the hanging and trailing plants are wonderful for clothing stark edges of planted raised beds, the edges of sills and so on. Hanging baskets give a well-filled look to the top of the conservatory roof space. You can use traditional hanging baskets, but they will need far less watering if you use succulents rather than the plants that are usually found in these containers. Look, too, at suspending pots with twisted wire loops. There are also some interesting 'ethnic' choices, such as macrame, which look very good and last a long time. You can buy raffia baskets that sit in the hangers.

## FOLIAGE HANGING AND CLIMBING PLANTS

### TRUE CACTI
*Pterocactus kuntzei* (see picture on p. 29) has tuberous, rooted, thin purple stems with an unusual dark, snaky appearance, so it makes an interesting container plant. It readily produces its yellow flowers, but be aware that it is a fragile, branching plant and sometimes breaks up. If this does happen, remember that the stems soon root and that they will provide you with more plants.

*Pterocactus tuberosus* (possibly a form of *P. kuntzei*) has trailing, thin, brown stems with very short spines and yellow flowers.

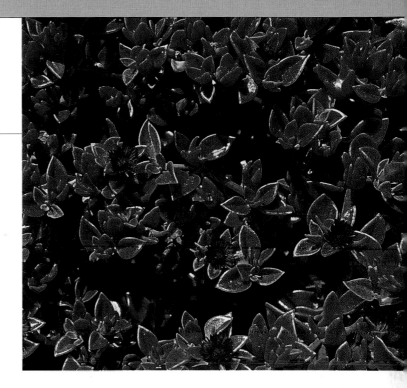

Blazing a trail: *Aptenia cordifolia* is an ideal plant for tall pots and hanging baskets.

## RHIPSALIS

These make lovely networks of plants. The delicate **filigree**-like growth is very attractive and can make a cloudy backdrop to many other plants. They are one of the epiphytic cacti, whose natural habit is to grow in the small pockets of food and moisture they can obtain in the forked branches of trees, so the habit of growth is pendant and branching. Because of their origins, they like rather more shade than other cacti.

There are several species to choose from, all of which bear tiny flowers in white or yellow, rather insignificant except *en masse*. The mistletoe cactus, or *Rhipsalis cereuscula,* has the additional attraction of white berries adorning its stems after flowering.

They are very easy to propagate from cuttings, so you can soon grow a large containerful. If you keep nipping the ends out of the new growth, setting them to one side for a couple of weeks to dry out and then pressing them into the pot or basket, you will have plenty of new growth.

*Rhipsalis cereuscula*, the rice or misteltoe cactus, has cascades of thin, bright green stems with cream flowers.

*Rhipsalis grandiflora* has cylindrical stems and whitish flowers striped green, rather larger than other rhipsalis species.

*Rhipsalis micrantha* is a robust trailing plant with four or five angled stems and small white flowers followed by round pink fruits.

*Rhipsalis pilocarpa* has narrow, branching stems with small cream flowers.

*Rhipsalis salicornioides* has thin, pendant, much-branched stems producing canary yellow flowers.

## OTHER SUCCULENTS

*Aptenia cordifolia* is a freely-branching leafy succulent bearing numerous purple-red flowers. It is good for hanging baskets, trailing over the edges of shelves and benches and in urn-shaped pots with a foot.

## CEROPEGIA

These are very useful plants. They have delicate foliage, often a lilac-grey colour, which is especially attractive and makes a good contrast to both green and purple-toned plants. This is a genus which enjoys a slightly more shaded location.

*Ceropegia woodii* is the species you are most likely to meet. Its attractive grey heart-shaped leaves have purple markings, and it bears small purple lantern-shaped flowers which appear very delicate and exotic.

*Ceropegia woodii variegata.*

of growth. It looks good in a hanging basket, because the basket itself will be well-filled, while the smaller plants at the end of arching stems makes an interesting shaggy cascade.

*Chlorophytum comosum* (reverse variegation) also has long, narrow leaves, variegated yellow and green, but with the yellow on the inside instead of the outside edges of the leaves.

CRASSULA

The mat-forming crassulas can be used in pots on shelving, where they soften the otherwise stark geometry of the display stand. They are also good in cascade pots (see Chapter 2 for construction details), where they can be used to spill over the edges. In beds in the conservatory they will give you rapid **ground cover**, and they will also work as underplanting in mixed pots and containers.

*Crassula lanuginosa* is a typical mat-forming species, with grey, pointed leaves which are softly hairy. It has small, white flowers.

*Crassula pellucida* subsp. *marginalis* is a really versatile choice, which will colour up into a spectacular maroon in the sunniest spot. Its leaves, which will become compressed and fatter, are **bi-coloured** maroon and green in slightly shaded conditions, becoming a rich, dark green in deeper shade. In all of its metamorphoses it will produce a mass of white flowers in the winter months.

*Crassula volkensii* is similar, but it has smaller leaves.

*Crassula peploides* is similar to *C. volkensi*, with a spreading habit and small green leaves tipped with red and white flowers.

*Ceropegia woodii* 'Variegata' is another excellent choice with its white-splashed leaves.

*Ceropegia ampliata* is the so-called leafless ceropegia, because it bears tiny leaves which drop off quite quickly. It is easy to flower, and has white flowers with green corolla lobes carried *en masse* in September.

*Ceropegia barklyi* is another delicate trailing plant with grey succulent leaves and lantern-shaped, purple flowers.

*Ceropegia bulbosa* has hanging, slender stems and leaves.

*Ceropegia sandersonii* is an easily grown climbing ceropegia. The green and white flowers with a cap are amongst the largest of the ceropegia flowers.

*Ceropegia stapeliiformis* also has large, greenish-white lantern-shaped flowers.

**Other species:**

*Chlorophytum comosum* is the familiar spider plant, so named because of the way its flowers form on long arching stems, as do its new little plantlets. The plant is not thought of as a succulent, but its roots, which are very thick, make it an easy-care, drought-resistant choice which will rapidly make lots

*Crassula pellucida* subsp. *marginalis.*

*Crassula peploides.*

*Kleinia repens.*

*Oscularia caulescens.*

*Kleinia repens* is another really useful succulent, with a mass of beautiful blue leaves and yellow flowers. It produces a clutch of thin fingers, which makes it a good plant for hanging or edging.

*Oscularia caulescens* has trailing stems, with thick triangular leaves with a grey bloom. Its flowers are pink and scented.

SEDUM
Another good genus with a range of interesting plants, which are remarkably unlike one another.

Donkeys' tails are some of the nicest and funniest succulent plants you can grow. They produce long, pendant 'tails', with overlapping leaves, like scales, giving the whole plant a really textured finish. These are lovely plants for strawberry pots or hanging containers, and they can also be grown along the length of a trough at the top of a wall to produce a magnificent curtain.

*Sedum burrito* is the smallest of the donkeys' tails, with trailing stems covered in small, egg-shaped green leaves. It has white flowers. This is a good choice for a tiny container such as a florist's stand.

ABOVE: *Sedum morganianum*,

BELOW: *Sedum sieboldii* f. *variegatum*.

*Sedum morganianum* is a larger version. It is a beautiful grey succulent trailing plant which makes a wonderful cascade in a strawberry pot or spilling out of the neck of a classical urn.

*Sedum morganianum* × *Echeveria derenbergii* is a choice hybrid. The echeveria part of its parentage gives the plant altogether larger, chunkier and more open 'tails', with cascades of succulent grey leaves terminating in clumps of yellowish flowers.

*Sedum ewersii* 'Nanum' is a trailing perennial with blue-grey leaves and red flowers.

*Sedum guatemalense* is a colourful plant with prostrate stems, bearing cylindrical and rounded green, yellow and red leaves and red flowers.

*Sedum lineare* 'Variegatum' is a mat-forming variegated plant with small narrow leaves, forming a pale green cloud. Good for hanging basket use.

*Sedum rubrum* is another colourful choice, with prostrate stems of grey-red succulent leaves. It has white flowers.

*Sedum sieboldii* is a really useful plant with delicate, arching stems up to 25cm (10in) long, bearing round turquoise-blue leaves and pink flowers.

*Sedum sieboldii* f. *variegatum* has arching stems with variegated cream and grey leaves and pink flowers.

STRING OF BEADS
These plants are also great fun. They make a dramatic trailing plant which lives up to its name – in time you can have a hanging basket with yards of trailing 'beads'. The plants thrive in slight shade, and they will

String of beads: *Senecio rowleyanus*.

benefit from plenty of water and feeding in the growing season, when they will fatten up into satisfying round beads – like children's 'popper beads' of years ago, or nice fat garden peas straight from the pod.

*Senecio herreanus* has green, slightly **elliptical**, bead-like leaves which are marked with translucent lines. It has white flowers.

*Senecio rowleyanus* is the classic string of beads with bright green bead-like leaves.

## MEDITERRANEAN SUCCULENTS FOR FOLIAGE AND FLOWER

These genera go together because they all have a similar habit and they are also found as reliable edging for beds and borders in Mediterranean gardens, where they are safe from frost. In the conservatory they make a good **evergreen** foliage choice, acting as a contrasting edging to beds planted up with tall specimens of, say, cereus, opuntia and columnar euphorbias: they are also excellent flowering choices for large containers. Because these plants are either half-hardy or hardy in milder areas they are also good for summer bedding in the garden, so plants in containers can go out in the summer if you want to ring the changes inside the conservatory.

*Carpobrutus acinaciformis* is a spreading succulent 15cm (6in) high, with stems trailing some 1.5m (5ft). It has curved, grey-green leaves with blister-like growths at the base and profuse purple-red flowers 12cm (5in) across.

*Carpobrutus deliciosus* has long, greyish-green leaves on creeping stems, and pinkish-purple flowers, 7–8cm (3in) in diameter. It has edible, spherical fig-like fruits.

*Carpobrutus edulis*, the Hottentot or Kaffir fig, has creeping stems with dull green leaves, about 6cm (2½in) in length and slightly inward curving. Its flowers, which are 8cm (3in) in diameter, are yellow at first, becoming flesh coloured or pink later. Again, it bears edible, spherical fruits.

*Disphyma crassifolium* is a creeping, mat-forming species, whose stems root very easily. It has short, tapering leaves, thick and dark green, 3cm (1in or so) long and 0.5cm (³⁄₁₆in) thick. Its pinkish-red flowers are 4cm (1½in) in diameter.

ABOVE: *Carpobrutus edulis.*   BELOW: *Disphyma crassifolium.*

ABOVE: *Lampranthus rosea*.
RIGHT: *Drosanthemum speciosum*.

*Dorotheanthus bellidiformis* (syn. *Mesembryanthemum criniflorum*) is one of the parents of the popular mesembryanthemum garden hybrids. It is mat-forming and bears large and numerous flowers coloured white, pale pink, red and orange.

*Dorotheanthus gramineus* (syn. *Mesembryanthemum tricolor*) has brilliant crimson flowers with a dark centre and a vigorous spreading habit.

*Drosanthemum bellum* is a loosely branching species, growing to 30cm (12in) tall with small and narrow cylindrical leaves. It bears large flowers, which are yellowish-pink with a white centre.

*Drosanthemum floribundum* forms a cushion of freely branching stems with small, succulent leaves, and produces masses of pale pink flowers.

*Drosanthemum speciosum* is a bushy shrub which can grow up to 60cm (2ft), but more generally reaches 30–40 cm (12–16in) in height and 30cm (12in) in spread, with erect, spotty stems and curved, almost cylindrical, succulent leaves 1.5cm (½in) long, with shiny **papillae**. It is particularly valued for its masses of bright solitary flowers, which are usually orange–red with green centres and reach 5cm (2in) across.

*Lampranthus copiosus* has spreading and branching stems with small, narrow leaves. Its large pink flowers have the advantage of staying open day and night.

*Lampranthus primivernus* has erect stems to 30cm (12in) tall with narrow leaves and loads of salmon pink flowers.

*Lampranthus rosea* is a bushy plant with thin, branching stems. It is highly prized for its abundant display of large lilac flowers.

*Lampranthus deltoides* is a small, spreading plant with triangular blue-green succulent leaves which have toothed reddish margins. It bears scented pink flowers in early summer.

*Lampranthus multiradiatus* is a small spreading shrub with narrow blue-green leaves and lilac flowers.

## HANGING PLANTS FOR FLOWER

### APOROCACTUS AND APOROPHYLLUM
Aporocacti are true species, while the aporophyllums are hybrids of aporocacti and

epiphyllums. Their common name of rats'
tails is an accurate description of the
aporocacti in particular, since they have long
and slender pendant stems bristling with
pale spines. The aporophyllums tend to have
rather fewer spines than the true species.

These plants are cacti and will flourish in a
frost-free conservatory in good light. They
need a winter rest, probably because this
dormant period triggers bud production.
They flower dependably, and make a
wonderful show with large flowers in
numerous pretty shades. Out of flower, the
long, hanging mass of trailing stems makes
for a very unusual hanging-basket display.

### True species:

*Aporocactus conzattii* has long, narrow
flowers in shades of red and maroon.

*Aporocactus flagelliformis* is the true rats'
tails, with deep pink to lilac flowers It is very
cold-tolerant, and it withstands many
degrees of frost if kept dry in the winter.

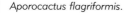

*Aporocactus flagriformis.*

All of the aporophyllum cultivars give
magnificent displays of flowers.

*Aporocactus
flagriformis* is a true
species with dark
crimson flowers.

*Aporocactus mallisonii*, also known
as *A. flagelliformis* var. *leptophis*, has
deep red flowers with a tinge of
maroon in the throat.

*Aporocactus martianus* has deep pink
flowers up to 10cm (4in) long.

### Aporophyllum cultivars:
'Beautie', flowers in shades of pink.
'Binkie', pale orangey pink with some yellow. Large.
'Caroline', bright orange to pink.
'Comptessa', large, orange-red flowers edged lilac.
'Dawn', shades of delicate pink, very
   large flowers.
'Brilliant', myriads of tubular red flowers.
'Edna Bellamy', large peachy red.
'Karen', large flame red.
'Lorna', shades of salmon pink and red.
'Maiden's Blush', large, pale pink flowers.
'Marsha', large flower, tints of orange and
   red shading to violet in the centre.
'Nadine', cerise-purple.
'Najla', orangey-red.
'Nicola', flame red.
'Pink Duchesse', very pale pink.
'Scheila', dark pink.
'Shirley', salmon pink .
'Susan', deep pink.
'Sussex Dawn', deep flesh pink.
'Sussex Peach', soft, peach-red flowers.
'Sussex Pink', peach with red stamens.
'Tangerine', deep orange.
'Vivide', very large red.
'Wendy', shades of pink and red.

*Aporophyullum
'Beautie'*

Christmas cactus.

CHRISTMAS CACTI

Also known as holiday cactus in USA, these really need no introduction, as they are so widely available. A large specimen makes a wonderful container, full of winter flowers, brightening the conservatory as a time when few other plants are blooming. They have characteristic zygomorphic flowers.

Ideally, individual pots should be given two plants back to back for an even potful of flowers, or you will find that you have a very assymetrical plant. They should be kept shaded from prolonged direct sunlight and watered just before the compost completely dries out, but they should not be given so much water that the compost remains saturated for long periods. You can feed them every two weeks or so. They like an **acid** soil, so they grow best in an **ericaceous** compost.

Although Christmas cacti are tolerant of low temperatures, down to about 2˚C (35˚F), at least for short periods, they should be kept above 7˚C (45˚F) if you want them to flower in the winter months. Some of the colours (e.g. white) develop pink flushing at lower temperatures, so they should be given temperatures of at least 12˚C (55˚F) to flower in their true shades.

The winter-flowering types are short day plants and need about ten hours of darkness to induce bud formation. Fortunately this condition arises naturally in the autumn, as long as exposure to strong artificial light is avoided during the night.

You will find that a wide colour range is available, and unnamed hybrids in pink and white, as well as the common purple-red variety, are readily found in supermarkets, DIY stores and garden centres etc. around Christmas. Ideally, the plants should not be moved once they have come into bud, so you may get a degree of flower drop, but these plants are generally successful purchases.

There are numerous named cultivars if you want a more certain colour outcome:

**Lilac/lavender/purple/cerise group**
*Schlumbergera* × *bridgesii* (syn. Christmas cactus), cerise flowers.
'Bristol Princess' (RHS award of merit). White or very pale pink mid-stripe on the petals, shading to pale lilac.
*Schlumbergera* × *buckleyi* (syn. the Christmas cactus), lilac to purple.

'Fabulous', large, light orchid pink.

'Garten Inspecktor Voll', ruby red.

'Mia', bushy species, orchid purple flowers.

*Schlumbergera obtusangula*, a rare species which looks like a miniature prickly pear cactus. Lilac flowers.

'Our Dolly', slim elegant lavender flowers, shading to white in the tube and at the base of the petals.

'Parma', purple-red, rounded petals.

'Purple Beauty', fuchsine purple flowers, freely produced.

'Purple Devil', bright orchid purple and red throughout.

'Rocket', fuchsine pink.

'Romance', beautiful lavender.

*Schlumbergera russelliana*, cerise.

'Tief Rosa', lilac-purple.

## Red/orange-red group

'Bicolor', orange and scarlet.

'Bristol Belle', rose pink shading to bright orange-red.

'Bristol Rose', cardinal red.

'Cavalier', vigorous plants. Flowers bright mid red with pink tube.

'Frankenstolz', one of the best old German cultivars. Scarlet with some lavender.

'Madame Ganna Walksa', cherry red with paler tube. Free-flowering.

'Norris', maroon.

'Red Devil, bright red.

'Red Elf', light red petals paling towards the centre, light purple tube.

'Rosea', Australian cultivar, cardinal red.

## Orange-red/salmon group

'Altensteinii', flowers large peach to orange, produced up to five times a year.

'Bon Ton', pale salmon orange with pale orchid tube. Free-flowering.

'Bristol Joy', large orange scarlet-flowers, sometimes with pink shades.

'Buenna Orange', mid orange-red petals, pale pink tube.

'Lucy', salmon, orange and purple.

'Oakleigh Festival', mid orange petals with a hint of gold. Fast-growing, free-flowering.

'Orange Devil', one of the brightest orange varieties, orchid purple tube.

'Sweet Sue', orange flower with pale orchid pink tube. Free-flowering.

'Weihnachtsfreude', free-flowering. The flowers are orange and pink with some magenta.

## Pink group

'Apricot', salmon pink.

'Pedca Beauty', lovely shell pink, living up to its name.

'Pink Lady', base of petals and tube are white, shading to lilac and pink at the edge of the petals.

'Westlands', bright pink.

## White and gold group

Note that the flower colour of these hybrids is temperature-dependent. They need temperatures of 12°C (55°F) and above, or they can show some pinkness on the base of the petals.

## White:

'Delicatus', white, sometimes with touch of pink.

'Snowflake', white.

'White Christmas', white, with pink at base of tube.

'White Dove', white flowers, flushed pink.

## Gold:

'Gold Charm', a very unusual and attractive warm gold flower, but unfortunately a much less vigorous grower than many of the other cultivars. It needs warmth, or a pink flushing will give it a nasty, muddy colour.

Orchid cactus.

### EASTER CACTI

As the name suggests, these have a later flowering cycle than the Christmas cacti, but in other respects they are largely the same. Known as holiday cacti in US.

'Elektra', large, lilac flowers.
*Schlumbergera gaertneri* (syn. *Rhipsalis gaertneri*) the Easter cactus, has large vermillion flowers.
'Mandy', flame red.
'Merlin', shades of deep pink to lilac.
*Rhipsalidopsis rosea*, a miniature plant with deep pink to lilac flowers.
'Scarborough', deep maroon with an unusual yellow throat.

### EPIPHYLLUM HYBRIDS (orchid cacti)

The name says it all with these fabulous plants. They have been extensively hybridized from their wild relatives, which grow in pockets of rotting vegetation in the crooks of forest branches.

Although they are cacti, the layman would not recognize them as such. Their long, pale strap-like 'leaves' are actually stems, and they have residual areoles with spines erupting from them. They are useful foliage in-fillers, either suspended from hanging baskets or wall containers, or tied to trellis, canes or other plant supports, but even devotees would hesitate to call them beautiful until they flower.

They produce massive, sometimes highly scented blooms reminiscent of the cup-shaped blooms you find on water lilies. They have been bred purely for the size and colour of their flowers, which are available in a wide range of shades. There is, however, no blue, which means that 'purple' has to be interpreted fairly loosely as a deep reddish hue – like the lilac red of the ubiquitous Christmas cactus.

It is important to consider the origins of the plants when potting them up. They are accustomed to meagre rations, so if they are given large containers with copious amounts of fertilizer-rich compost they will imagine they have been transported to heaven: they will make luxuriant vegetative growth, but will see no reason to flower because they are under no stress to reproduce.

The trick, therefore, is to underpot them in a fairly gritty soil-based compost, to weigh them down and prevent them toppling over. They like a shady position, but don't overwater them and certainly don't feed them. This treatment should trigger flower in the spring and early summer. Only after they have exhausted themselves by this floral display should you water and feed them generously, repotting them once they are showing obvious signs of recovery.

Do label your plants well because out of flower they are completely indistinguishable from one another. We have learned this to our literal cost in the nursery: lose a label from a seed tray of cuttings and the plants are completely worthless!

## True species

These are some of the parent plants which have been used in hybridization:

*Cryptocereus anthonyanus* syn. *Selenicereus anthonyanus*, creamy-white 12cm (5in) long flowers.

*Epiphyllum crenatum*, white, slightly fragrant.

*E. lepidocarpum*, white, night-bloomer.

*E. oxypetalum*, large, fragrant white night-bloomer: true species, frequently called queen of the night, although this title is more usually given to the selenicereus (see below).

'Deutsche Kaiserine', which is actually *Nopalxochia phyllanthoides*. This has beautiful shell pink flowers and a mass of small blooms.

*Selenicereus testudo*, true species; large white to cream blooms.

## Cultivars

### Bi-colours

'Anthon Gunther', multi-coloured carmine red, orange and purple.

'Astronaut', multi-coloured purple, red and pink.

'Bohemienne', small-growing type with small flowers in shades of pink, purple and white.

'Curt Backeberg', multi-coloured blooms, with orange mid-stripe and purple edges. Extra-large flowers: spectacular.

'Dante', beautiful wide-open flowers with lavender pink inner petals with purple mid-stripe and purple outer petals, tinged with orange and red. Strongly perfumed.

'Denis Kucera', flat open petals of orange and violet: extra-large flowers.

'Dr Werdermann', open cup-shaped flowers in purple, with orange stripe and orchid edges.

'Dracula', extra-large flowers; open cup of purple, with a red mid-stripe and dark red outer petals and sepals.

'Duchesse', purple, maroon and white. Very large, attractive flowers.

'Frau Wegener', pale violet cup with a saucer of deep carmine. Large.

'Hans Rehm', blood red edged with rose.

'Indian Chief', red-orange with purple edge to inner petals.

'Jenkinsonii', scarlet with orange-red mid-stripe and violet in the throat. Very large easily produced flowers.

'Lydia', very nice lilac on most of petal shading to maroon on extreme edges.

'Nell Gwynn', lilac, pink and rose.

'Patience', shell pink shading to white at centre of petals. Very impressive .

'Paula Knebel', dark red outer petals, purple-red inner petals with pale lilac edges. Large and very impressive.

'Pride of Bell', white with rose and orchid striping the petals and most of the sepals; large flowers with long thin sepals.

'Rosalita', purplish rose and lavender off-season bloomer on dwarf growth; small flowers.

'Space Rocket', very large, wide-open flowers with lilac centre petals and magenta outer petals with a deeper mid-rib.

'Wanderlust', ruffled dark pink flowers with cherry eye. Large.

Pocket calculators: in their natural habitat these epiphytes take advantage of pockets of nutrients in the stone.

## Oranges

'Amber Queen', deep flame orange.

'Best of All', deep orange flushed with fuchsine.

'Chelford Royal', salmon to orange.

'Day in Spring', salmon orange.

'Denis Kucera', flat open petals of orange and violet: extra-large flowers.

'Desert Sunrise', orange edged with fuchsine purple.

'G. M. Peach', shades of pink and peach.

'Holy Wells', bright orange.

'Indian Fox', burnt orange.

'Orange Princess', orange.

'Sun Goddess', old favourite with huge orange flowers.

## Pinks

'Celesto', very pale pink.

'Crinoline Lady', free-flowering, pale orange-pink.

'Empress', small pink flowers. Small-growing type.

'Euphrosine', rose pink, cup-and-saucer shape; medium to large flowers.

'Fawn', salmon, edged with soft rose pink.

'Fortuna', delicate pink.

'J. T. Barber', deep salmon pink.

'Jaybee', two-tone pink with a deeper mid-rib.

'Lady Irene', orchid pink, large and fragrant.

'London Lady', shrimp pink: medium-sized.

'London Magic', deep pink funnel-shaped blooms; medium-sized flowers.

'Mignonette', very small rose pink flowers.

'Nilmah', rose pink with a lavender eye.

'Orchis', buff to pink.

'Padre', lavender pink; large, open flowers; reliable.

'Patience', shell pink shading to white at centre of petals. Very impressive.

'Pink Nymph', outstanding small, pink-flowered variety. Late bloomer.

'Professor Ebert', lilac and pink: reliable old favourite.

## Purples

'Ballyshavel', deep lilac and purple.

'Blau Flamme', purple flowers: light, almost white, margins.

'Chiapora', lilac.

'Gigantea', purple.

'Lilac Time', deep lilac ruffled flower.

'London Fog', unusual smoky lavender rose flowers.

'Lydia', very nice lilac on most of petal, shading to maroon on the extreme edges.

'Midnight', dark purple outer petals, lilac inner petals.

'Purple Delight', violet-purple inner petals, purple-red outer petals. Large.

'Recluse', fantastic, with very large purple flowers which shade to maroon in the petal centres.

'Royal Robe', cherry purple and lilac over pink.

## Reds

'Ackermanii', very free-flowering funnel-form orange-red blooms. An old favourite with long-lasting flowers.

'Apache', bright orange-red flowers.

'Bacchus', vivid red.

'Conway's Giant', large red flowers with slight purple at centre and at the edges of the petals. A reliable flowerer. Perfumed.

'Eastern Crimson', vivid crimson.

'El Indio Tomatorea', orange-red.

'Ignescens', large light orange-red flowers with slightly ruffled petals.

'Jungle Moon', very deep red with slight touches of purple on the edges of the petals. Large flowers.

'Red Kaiserine', small, bright red flowers, with slight maroon on petal edges.

'Red Velvet', velvety dark red petals: fragrant. Extra large.

'Red Wing', deep Chinese red. Extra large.

'Rotkaeppchen', (German for Red Riding Hood), attractive small orange-red flowers.

'Scarle', deep red shading to purple in the centre. Large.

'Vive Rouge', vivid red shading to orange at centre; purple filaments.

### Whites

'Alba Superba', cream.

'Argentii', small white flowers.

'Cooperi', old favourite: highly scented white flowers with yellow outer petals.

'Eden', free-flowering white and yellow.

'Forstein', white centre, cream outer petals; scented.

'Gardenia', highly scented cream flowers.

'Kinchinjunga', cream and white.

'London Moonlight', creamy-white.

'Petite Cherie', small white flowers.

'Phantom', large white flowers.

'Polar Bear', white petals with lemon tips.

'Roseopurpureus', white veined with purple.

'San Jacinto', narrow white inner petals: brownish-white back petals; extra-large flowers.

'Sunland', creamy-white.

'White Queen', large white and cream scented flowers.

### Yellows

'Discovery', clear yellow.

'Dobson's Yellow', free-flowering creamy-yellow.

'Golden Dreams', large golden flowers with a purple eye.

'Orial', creamy-yellow.

'Reward', rich, soft yellow; wide-open large flowers.

'Sunburst', gold with white eye.

## HOYA

These are fabulous evergreen climbing and/or trailing plants grown for their exotic waxy flowers and dark green glossy foliage. They make wonderful conservatory and indoor subjects in a slightly shaded position, so give them some shade in the summer. Apart from *Hoya carnosa* and *H. kuhlii*, they need to be kept warmer than most of the other succulents – around 10˚F (50˚C) upwards – so they will not flourish in a conservatory which is only kept frost-free.

They like a rich, well-drained soil, with moderate watering in full growth, water sparingly otherwise.

*Hoya australis* is an easily grown climbing plant which flowers well in the spring. It has white, highly scented flowers.

*Hoya carnosa* is the best-known and most widely available of the hoyas, with climbing stems with thick, succulent leaves. It bears amazing pale pink flowers in clusters. The waxy texture and intricate detail of the flower heads make them appear almost artificial, especially as the flowers are so long-lasting. Along with *H. kuhlii*, it is the most cool-tolerant of the hoyas.

*Hoya carnosa.*

Pride of place: a *Hoya linearis* can be seen at the top right of this conservatory hanging and trailing arrangement.

*Hoya biakensis* is a very attractive species, with green leaves mottled with white, and with small yellow flowers.

*Hoya bilobata* is very useful as it produces **umbels** of small red flowers all year round.

*Hoya diversifolia* has mottled leaves and with flowers in waxy clusters, like *H. carnosa*, but which can vary in colour.

*Hoya heusckeliana* carries unusual pinkish red ball-shaped flowers.

*Hoya imperialis* is a large climbing plant, producing flowers about 7.5cm (3in) in diameter, but it does need to be kept particularly warm in winter at 17˚–18˚C (64˚F).

*Hoya kerrii* is one of the easiest hoyas to recognize, with its thick, leathery, heart-shaped leaves. It is a climber which, when it is large enough, has the advantage of being free-flowering.

*Hoya kuhlii* is mainly a trailing plant, but it will also climb. The flowers are pink with a red centre. Like *H carnosa* it is more cool-tolerant than most hoyas.

*Hoya linearis* produces cascades of narrow leaves and pendant, waxy white flowers. Like *H. carnosa* and *H. kuhlii* it is more cool tolerant than most hoyas.

*Hoya pauciflora* will hang or climb. It has thin leaves and single white flowers.

*Hoya pseudo-littoralis* bears scented white flowers with pink centres in the spring.

*Hoya sussuelea* has large flesh-coloured flowers and is easy to grow.

*Hoya thomsonii* is an attractive hanging plant with dark green hairy leaves. It is very attractive when in flower, as it bears highly scented white flowers.

KALANCHOE
These kalanchoes are nothing like the mass-produced, almost perpetually flowering pot plants found in supermarkets all year round. Instead they are loosely trailing, leafy plants with pretty and profuse flowers.

*Kalanchoe manginii* is a superb trailing plant with narrow stems and pendant bell-shaped red flowers.

*Kalanchoe* 'Mirabella' has flowers with approximately 2cm (⅞in) long red petals and a yellow tube.

*Kalanchoe* 'Wendy' is a lovely plant, ideal for hanging baskets. It is semi-erect with glossy green leaves, and bears long-lasting 2cm (⁷⁄₈in) long, bell-shaped, pinkish-red flowers with yellow tips in late winter.

## SELENICEREUS: 'QUEEN OF THE NIGHT' CACTI

These are slender-stemmed, trailing cacti from South America, and they are well-known for their very large and showy flowers – the finest and largest of all the cacti. They are mostly night-flowering, with the buds opening in all their glory towards sunset and in some cases saturating the air around them with their fragrance. They are particularly beautiful when seen by artificial light.

*Selenicereus boeckmannii* has richly perfumed yellow and white flowers, up to 20cm (8in) across.

*Selenicereus coniflorus* has white inner petals surrounded by yellow curved outer petals. The flowers are up to 25cm (10in) across.

*Selenicereus grandiflorus* has pure white petals surrounded by yellow sepals forming a large globular cup up to 30cm (12in) across. It has a strong vanilla perfume.

*Kalanchoe* 'Wendy'.

*Selenicereus hallensis* has huge white and yellow flowers with a vanilla perfume.

*Selenicereus nelsonii* has pure white flowers up to 25cm (10in) long and markedly fragrant.

*Selenicereus pteranthus* has large creamy-white flowers which are strongly perfumed.

*Selenicereus spinulosus* has white flowers backed with reddish sepals.

*Kalanchoe* 'Mirabella'.

# CHAPTER 9
# FLOWERING PLANTS

Many people think of cacti in terms of spiny spheres and columns, but if you select the right genera you will find that they offer a magnificent display of flowers in spring

Magnificent seven: *Schwantesia herrei* in the centre with (top left, clockwise) *Chamaecereus silvestrii* hybrid, *Lobivia pentlandii*, *Gymnocalycium baldianum*, *Chamaecereus silvestrii* 'Yellow Bird', *Lobivia wrightiana* and *Chamaecereus silvestrii* hybrid white.

All cacti will flower eventually, but some of them have to be so large that their flowers are unlikely to be seen, except in habitat or perhaps in the large glasshouses of botanical gardens. Therefore the smaller cacti, which quickly reach maturity in cultivation, are the ones to go for – and once they have reached the necessary size, they will produce blooms reliably year after year with only the minimum of care and attention.

For regular flower, cacti need a dry spell over the winter – a spell of dormancy to produce their buds. Watering should therefore be reduced gradually in the autumn in order to rest the plants during the winter. If your plants are kept in an unheated porch or conservatory, they need to be kept free from frost – at around 5˚C (40˚F) – and they should be kept completely dry from around late autumn to early spring. In a warmer situation, indoors or in a heated conservatory, you may find that you need to mist the plants occasionally to prevent them from shrivelling, but less is always more with these plants, so be sparing.

In spring, gradually build up the watering, until the plants are being watered once or twice a week by the summer. They also appreciate feeding every two or three weeks. If you look closely at your plants from late winter to early spring onwards, you will see tiny tufts forming on your cacti. These will gradually swell until they form obvious flower buds.

You can pot your flowering cacti separately, but they do make a fabulous show in containers, and a bowl garden of flowering cacti is easily as welcome in the spring as a pot of daffodils or hyacinths, and far more unusual. Once you have set it up, that's more or less all you have to do in order to provide an annual show. This means that these are ideal containers to bring into a prominent position in the house when they are at their best, and they can be popped back into relative obscurity afterwards.

Genera to look for are those which are are compact and flower readily when small.

### CHAMAECEREUS

Chamaecereus (also known as chamaelobivia) are also known as peanut cacti because of their segmented habit. It is common now to regard the chamaecereus genus as absorbed into lobivia, but (as explained in the introduction) I am treating them separately here because the hybrids are so distinctive in their own right.

The species is *C. silvestrii*, which has a pale green body, forming finger-like clumps and carrying large scarlet flowers. It is a sturdy grower. However, plant breeders have also concentrated on this genus to produce a number of attractive and large-flowered hybrids with a choice of white, yellow and orange flowers.

*Chamaecereus silvestrii* var. *cristate* is the 'deformed' version, with thickened, stems ending in a flattened, club-like cristate head. It has scarlet flowers like the species.

*Chamaecereus silvestrii* var. *pectinifera* forms clumps, with long, stout cylindrical stems and large, readily produced orange-red flowers.

*Chamaecereus silvestrii* 'Andy' is a a robust columnar plant with attractive gold flowers.

*Chamaecereus silvestrii* 'Greenpeace' has pale yellow flowers with a pretty green mid-stripe.

*Chamaecereus silvestrii* 'Ragged Robin' is particularly worth hunting out. As the name suggests, its purple-red flowers have 'ragged' petals like the wild flower of the same name.

*Chamaecereus silvestrii* 'Sunset' has an abundance of orange and red flowers.

*C silvestrii* 'Yellow Bird' is an unusual yellow-flowered hybrid.

You will also come across numerous unnamed cultivars, including at least one white-flowered form and a pretty lilac.

*Echinocereus pentalophus.*

## ECHINOCEREUS

Echinocereus is a large-flowered genus of more than 70 species of showy plants, many with attractive spines, which bear colourful flowers up to 12cm (5in) across. These plants can give diversity to a collection because they grow in a variety of shapes, and they can be globular, columnar or trailing. Their flowers come mainly in shades of yellow, orange, pink and purple and have the advantage that they are frequently long-lived.

*Echinocereus berlandieri* is a branching plant, which soon forms a prostrate clump of cylindrical stems. It has large, long-lasting pink flowers.

*Echinocereus pentalophus* has long thick stems, which are pale green, and have a sprawling habit. The flowers are very showy, growing up to 12cm (5in) long, and coloured lilac or pink with a white throat.

Close relations: there are numerous unnamed hybrids of *Chamaecereus silvestrii*, as well as named cultivars such as 'Yellow Bird' (below right).

*Echinocereus polyacanthus* is a showy plant, with long needle-like spines. It can form a mat-like growth with up to 50 heads. It has large, funnel-shaped, carmine flowers.

*Echinocereus reichenbachii* var. *baileyi* has attractive white spines, which are tinged pink, and large, light purple flowers.

*Echinocereus triglochidiatus* has sparse, but long white and black spines and long-lasting deep red flowers.

*Echinocereus viridiflorus* is a freely offsetting species, with unusual and attractive yellowish-green flowers.

ECHINOPSIS
These are easily grown plants, often clustering with age. Most species have spectacular and very large tubular flowers, which are often perfumed and which open at night.

*Echinopsis* 'Green Gold' has pale yellow perfumed flowers, usually opening in the evening.

*Echinopsis ancistrophora* has large 15cm (6in) long flowers with green outer petals and white inner ones.

*Echinopsis ancistrophora* subsp. *cardenasiana* has masses of large glossy magenta flowers.

*Echinopsis ancistrophora* subsp. *pojoensis* is a fresh green plant with large, orange-red flowers.

*Echinopsis eyriesii* is a reliable bloomer, with huge white flowers up to 25cm (10in) long.

*Echinopsis* 'Gerrits Lemon' has pretty, pale yellow flowers.

*Echinopsis* 'Haku Jo' is a cultivar of Japanese origin, which has an attractive blue-green body with amazing felted ribs. It bears large, white, strongly perfumed flowers with narrow, curving petals.

*Echinopsis obrepanda* has readily produced white, pink or purple flowers.

*Echinopsis oxygona* has very large pink flowers.

*Echinopsis silvestrii* readily produces incredible, 20cm (8in) long, pure white flowers. Has to be seen to be believed!

Like the chamaecereus, the echinopsis have attracted the attention of plant breeders, so it is worth hunting out the 'Paramount hybrids' which have been bred for their huge, brightly coloured flowers.

Triplets: the three plants on the left are echinocereus species, those on the right echinopsis species.

## GYMNOCALYCIUM

This is an excellent group for the beginner or advanced collector because it offers such a wide variety of form, spination, flower and colour. There are more than 60 species in all, and these are some of the prettiest for flower:

*Gymnocalycium achiransense* is olive green with many stout spines. It has lovely white flowers flushed with pink, often growing larger than the plant.

*Gymnocalycium ambatoense* is a globular species, up to 15cm (6in) across, with powerful, curving straw-coloured spines. Large white flowers with pink mid-stripe.

*Gymnocalycium baldianum* is a dark grey to bluish green plant bearing magnificent flowers in shades of red and maroon. It is one of the best gymnocalyciums.

*Gymnocalycium bodenbenderianum* is beautiful whether in or out of bloom. It has attractive spines, which give this purple-grey plant the appearance of a sea urchin. It produces pure white flowers.

*Gymnocalycium bruchii* is a choice miniature, clustering species with pretty lilac flowers.

*Gymnocalycium damsii* is deep-green, often tinged red or brown, with large pink flowers.

*Gymnocalycium denudatum* has sparse, strong, curved spines and large, glossy white or pink flowers.

*Gymnocalycium horridispinum* is noteworthy for its long, stout and very striking spines and its large pink and white flowers, which remain open for a week.

*Gymnocalycium intertextum* is greyish-green with attractive long, tangled spines and white flowers.

*Gymnocalycium leptanthemum* has extra-long white flowers.

*Gymnocalycium mesapotamicum* has shining green stems, with thin, curving spines and large pale pink flowers.

*Gymnocalycium mostii* is an attractive, bluish-green plant with strong, curving, grey spines. It carries large pink flowers, up to 8cm (over 3in) across.

*Gymnocalycium multiflorum* is a bright green plant, eventually clumping, with flattened, curved yellow spines. It has pretty bell-shaped pink flowers shading to almost white.

*Gymnocalycium piltziorum* is a flattened, globular plant, grey or grey-green in colour, with powerful spines. It bears large pink flowers.

*Gymnocalycium platense* and *G. quehlianum* both have strikingly attractive white flowers with contrasting red throats.

*Gymnocalycium ritterianum* is an attractive plant with long, stout and curved cream-coloured spines and large, pure-white flowers.

*Gymnocalycium stellatum* has an unusual olive green to grey-green body which has brown or black spines and carries large, pure white flowers.

Twins: *Gymnocalycium baldianum* and *G. multiflorum*.

LEFT TO RIGHT
*Lobivia backebergii* subsp. *wrightiana.*
*Lobivia pentlandii.*

## LOBIVIA

Easy to grow, these compact globular plants have large flowers in dazzling reds, yellows, pinks and white - often in strongly contrasting colours with darker centres.

*Lobivia arachnacantha* is a small clumping plant with huge glossy purple flowers that are often often bigger than the plant itself.

*Lobivia aurea* is a white-spined plant with attractive, two toned, lemon yellow flowers with deep yellow centres.

*Lobivia aurea* var. *dobeana* is a clumping species. Its amazing red flowers have contrasting bright yellow centres.

*Lobivia backebergii* subsp. *wrightiana* is a desirable species with pale cerise flowers.

*Lobivia chrysantha* subsp. *jajoiana* has elongating plant bodies. Probably the best species for really flashy flowers, as it has readily produced beaker-shaped wine red or pink flowers with dramatic black centres.

*Lobivia hertrichiana* has attractive, very dark red flowers.

*Lobivia haematantha* var. *amblayensis* is only 2cm × 3cm (around an inch high and wide), although it is often clumping in cultivation. It has large flowers 6–10cm (2½–4in) across in yellow or orange.

*Lobivia pentlandii* is a dark, grey-green plant with large flowers which come in an astonishing range of colours – yellow, orange, pink, violet or red.

## MAMMILLARIA

The genus mammillaria contains over 300 species and is the most popular of all groups of cacti. Some of the species are excellent for flowers which are produced in the form of a ring around the top of the plant and are succeeded by fleshy red seedpods, giving the plant an interesting appearance throughout the winter.

*Mammillaria bocasana* is an attractive clustering species, appealing out of flower as well as in, with masses of white wool and white spines. It has cream flowers, followed by bright red seedpods.

LEFT TO RIGHT: *Lobivia arachnacantha, Lobivia aurea* var. *dobeana, Lobivia hertrichiana* and *Lobivia haematantha* var. *amblayensis.*

*Mamillaria laui* f. *subducta*.

*Mammillaria bombycina* has pretty, light carmine red flowers, red seedpods and the bonus of very attractive spines.

*Mammillaria boolii* is a choice species covered in glassy-white spines, some of them hooked. It also bears large orange flowers.

*Mammillaria fraileana* is a cylindrical plant with white flowers which are flushed pink and are produced in a ring near the crown of the plant.

*Mammillaria geminispina* is a freely offsetting plant, which forms cushions of plants. It has stiff white spines and attractive bi-coloured flowers, which are cream with carmine centres.

*Mammillaria glassii* var. *ascensionis* has many advantages: it is a rapidly clumping species, covered in attractive, fluffy white spines, and is one of the earliest to bloom. The flowers are an attractive pink.

*Mammillaria laui* has yellow spines and magenta flowers.

*Mamillaria laui* f. *subducta* is densely covered in cream or white spines and has deep pink flowers.

*Mammillaria longiflora* is notable for its large white and pink flowers.

*Mammillaria longimamma* has long, bright green tubercles and large yellow flowers, readily produced in the early spring.

*Mammillaria zeilmanniana* is one of the best mammillarias for a long and showy display of flowers. This superb freely flowering species has rings of lilac flowers and makes a fabulous show.

*Mammillaria zeilmanniana* var. *alba* is like its parent, but with rings of white flowers. Mix them together for an eye-watering display.

LEFT TO RIGHT: *Mammillaria boolii* and *Mammillaria zeilmanniana*.

LEFT: *Neoporteria subgibbosa.*
RIGHT: *Neoporteria villosa.*

## NEOPORTERIA

These have interesting bodies which are often coloured red-brown, olive-green and other unusual tones, with interesting spination. They usually have pretty pink flowers, which appear almost throughout the year (in the late autumn and the early spring, as well as in the early summer) so they are useful for extra flower.

*Neoporteria subgibbosa* is grey-spined with pretty pink and white flowers.

*Neoporteria villosa* grows into a striking dark green, almost black, plant with grey spines and magenta flowers.

*Neoporteria wagenknechtii* has dark grey or brown bodies and purple flowers.

## NOTOCACTUS

Notocactus is a deservedly popular genus of globular or short columnar plants with a range of spination. Their showy flowers, usually bright yellow, are reliably produced.

*Notocactus acutus* has large yellow flowers with yellow centres.

*Notocactus buiningii* is attractive even when not in flower because of its light, grass green colour, symmetrical ribs and spination. It also has very large, yellow flowers.

*Notocactus graessneri* is a popular, yellow-spined, yellow-flowered species.

*Notocactus haselbergii* is a lovely, small-growing species, which is entirely covered with soft white to yellow spines. It has long-lasting, unusual fiery red flowers.

*Notocactus herteri* is noteworthy for its fine, glossy, deep purplish-red flowers.

*Notocactus laetivirens* produces its pretty yellow flowers even when quite small.

*Notocactus muricatus* has white or yellow spines and large sulphur yellow flowers.

*Notocactus oxycostatus* is an outstanding species, with large, very white areoles around the glossy reddish-brown spines. It has bell-shaped yellow flowers.

*Notocactus rutilans* is an unusual and choice species. The flowers are large and carmine-coloured, shading to yellow and white in the throat.

*Notocactus schlosseri* has lovely glossy, lemon yellow flowers with a light green mid-stripe.

*Notocactus scopa* var. *candidus* is a lovely, deservedly popular species, which is entirely covered in soft white spines. It has large, canary yellow flowers.

*Notocactus tabularis* has large glossy yellow flowers with a carmine throat.

*Notocactus uebelmannianus* is a very fine looking, glossy, dark green cactus, with attractive wavy spines which are flattened against the plant and sometimes interlacing. It bears glossy, wine red flowers.

## PARODIA

This is a genus containing more than 90 species and including some of the most free-flowering and attractive of the globular cacti. They are often slow-growing for the first year and then become more vigorous.

*Parodia aureispina* has dense, hooked, honey yellow to reddish-brown spines. It produces its flowers readily in spring/early summer. It is a bit of an oddity in that it has two forms which are identical except that one has orange-red flowers and the other yellow.

*Parodia culpinensis* has an attractive body, with spiralling ribs covered in white wool and brown curved spines. It bears red flowers.

*Parodia dichroacantha* has white fluffy areoles and a woolly top. This is another species which has either large red or red and yellow flowers.

*Parodia herzogii* are attractive plants with very long white interlacing spines and large golden yellow to orange flowers.

*Parodia laui* is a superb species with fabulous glossy flowers, which are salmon reddish, tipped carmine, shading to yellow, orange and red.

*Parodia maassii* has large coppery-yellow flowers. It has strong, curved spines.

*Parodia microsperma* is a larger parodia which grows up to 20cm (8in) high and 10cm (4in) in diameter. It has thin white spines and large yellow flowers.

*Parodia mutabilis* is one of the most handsome of parodias, with large golden yellow flowers.

*Parodia otuyensis* has a greyish-green body and unusual carmine flowers with petals bordered violet or brownish-yellow.

*Parodia rubristaminea* is a globular species, up to 5cm (12in) across, with white spines and numerous, large, deep yellow flowers.

*Parodia sanguiniflora* has spiral ribs covered in fine, white, bristly spines. It carries large, bright red, glossy flowers.

*Parodia spegazziniana* is a solitary but imposing species, growing to 9cm (22in) high by 7cm (17in) with red flowers about 5cm (12in) across.

*Parodia subtilihamata* has unusual golden orange flowers with pink throats.

*Parodia tarabucina* is a fine species with salmon to purple flowers.

*Parodia aureispina* – yellow and orange-red flowered forms.

## REBUTIA

Rebutias are one of the best groups for bright, colourful flowers, and if you have limited space this is the most easily grown and flowered genus which no collection should be without. They are compact, globular, clump-forming plants, with generally softer bristle-like spines, which makes them easier to handle than some of the fiercer genera.

The flowers come in a range of colours, including white, red, yellow, and apricot. A collection of rebutias in the spring is a wonderful sight, forming a dazzling carpet of flowers. Each plant is very free-flowering: a single one can completely hide itself in 30 or more flowers.

*Rebutia fabrisii* is a readily clumping species which forms mounds of small heads covered in white spines. It has yellow flowers.

*Rebutia fiebrigii* has dense white spines and deep, velvety red flowers.

*Rebutia heliosa* × *albiflora* is a choice clustering plant, with attractive spines and peach and white flowers.

*Rebutia hoffmanii* is a clustering, greyish-green plant, with soft, bristly, white spines. Its orange flowers have a tinge of pale lavender.

*Rebutia kieslingii* has large orange flowers with white throats.

*Rebutia marsoneri* is a highly desirable species with bright golden yellow flowers.

*Rebutia minuscula* var. *violaciflora* has large and magnificent lilac-purple flowers.

*Rebutia narvaecensis* is a fine species covered in white spines and having masses of light pink to lilac flowers.

*Rebutia pseudodeminuta* has beautiful maroon flowers produced in large numbers.

*Rebutia pulvinosa* is a miniature gem with bright orange flowers.

*Rebutia pygmaea* is greyish or bluish green, with flowers in shades of pink and maroon.

*Rebutia senilis* has dense pure white spines and flame red flowers.

LEFT TO RIGHT: *Rebutia heliosa ×
albiflora, Rebutia hoffmanii,
Rebutia minuscula* var. *violaciflora*
and *Rebutia xanthocarpa*.

*Sulcorebutia
crispata*.

*Rebutia senilis* 'Rose of York' is a choice
cultivar with large white flowers.

*Rebutia spegazziniana* has maroon flowers
appearing much later than most rebutias, so
this is a good choice for a succession of
flower.

*Rebutia wessneriana* var. *krainziana* displays
very thin and short snow white spines set
against a dark green body, giving it an
attractive appearance. It has intensely red
or yellow flowers.

*Rebutia xanthocarpa* has carmine flowers.

*Rebutia xanthocarpa* f. *citricarpa* has striking
flowers in shades of pink.

*Setiechinopsis mirabilis*. These are
remarkable, brown-purple, plants with mop-
head cream flowers on a very long stem. The
flowers are perfumed and open at night. This
is a very easy species to grow and flower.

## SULCOREBUTIA

These plants are globular and generally
clump-forming. They are collected for their
interesting spines and for their numerous
large flowers, which come in a variety of
vivid, glossy colours, almost fluorescent in
their intensity. Like most of the flowering
cacti, these plants grow well from seed.

*Sulcorebutia candiae* has large deep yellow
flowers.

*Sulcorebutia crispata* is a grey-green plant
with white to red-brown spines which are
curved and curling into the stem. It has large
and stunning dark magenta flowers.

*Sulcorebutia frankiana* is an olive green plant
with large, glossy maroon flowers.

*Sulcorebutia menesesii* is a choice plant, with
attractive curly spines and golden yellow
flowers.

LEFT: *Sulcorebutia candiae*.
RIGHT: *Sulcorebutia menesesii*.

FACING PAGE, LEFT TO RIGHT:
*Rebutia marsoneri*.
*Rebutia pulvinosa*.
*Rebutia senilis*.

*Thelocactus bicolor.*

*Sulcorebutia mentosa* has shiny dark green stems which produce numerous rich purple flowers.

*Sulcorebutia pampagrandensis* is a beautifully spined plant, grey-green in colour with violet tints. It has fabulous, large, purple flowers with pink throats.

*Sulcorebutia pulchra* is one of the most charming species, with thin, wispy spines and a strongly clustering habit. It has large, funnel-shaped flowers in lilac-red.

*Sulcorebutia rauschii* has a green or purple body with black or gold spines and lilac-red flowers.

*Sulcorebutia steinbachii* has a green body, forming broad, cushion-like groups from a tap root. The spines may at first be absent on cultivated plants. They have scarlet flowers.

*Sulcorebutia tiraquensis* var. *electracantha* is a clumping species covered in white spines, with orange to red flowers.

*Sulcorebutia vasqueziana* has an unusual blackish-green to violet-black body, with weak, tangled golden-yellow to reddish spines. The flowers are pretty, in magenta or red, and yellow inside.

## THELOCACTUS

Look, too, for thelocacti, which are small, globular plants, often with interesting spination. They are free-flowering, in a range of colours including white, pink, red, yellow and lilac, with glossy petals. Some have an almost continuous stream of flowers from the late spring onwards.

*Thelocactus bicolor* has attractively coloured spines, in contrasting red and brown, and large, deep pink flowers.

*Thelocactus setispinus* has a strongly ribbed body and yellow flowers produced in sequence from summer through the autumn.

*Thelocactus tulensis* is a dramatic brown plant with long grey spines. The magnificent white flowers have a pink midstripe.

*Weingartia neocumingii* is a dramatic plant, with a dark green or black body, growing up to 20cm (8in) high and 10cmn (4in) across. It bears bright golden yellow flowers.

## FREE-FLOWERING OTHER SUCCULENTS

Good flowering choices which are also important for structure, leaf colour, in-filling or just for curiosity value are treated in detail elsewhere, and the hanging flowering choices have been covered thoroughly in Chapter 8.

*Sulcorebutia mentosa.*
*Sulcorebutia tiraquensis var. electracantha.*

It is worth remembering, however, the bonus offered by some of the other plants in terms of their flowers. As well as their really colourful leaves, for example, echeverias have bright yellow or red flowers produced on long, curving stalks in the summer.

Succulents also offer a great deal of scope for 'off peak' flowering, which gives the possibility of a mixed conservatory, with traditional flowering choices like petunias and busy lizzies for the summer months and some more unusual choices for the winter months. These species also give welcome flowers indoors during the dreary and relatively flower-free winter period. Most crassulas, for example, are good for winter flower, producing masses of starry white flowers. Lithops, conophytums and the other living stones (see Chapter 10) produce white, yellow, pink and purple daisy-like flowers in the autumn which are almost ridiculously large and showy for such tiny plants.

*Cotyledon orbiculata* has a superb grey bloom on the leaves and carries red and yellow flowers on a long stalk.

*Cotyledon orbiculata.*

*Cotyledon undulata* has thick leaves covered in a grey bloom and, as the Latin suggests, the leaves have distinctly wavy edges, sometimes with a red tinge. This plant produces orange-red flowers on a long stalk.

CRASSULA
*Crassula ausiensis* is a compact, branching plant, with grey, hairy leaves and white flowers.

*Crassula cooperi* is a fine miniature, flowering profusely in winter.

*Crassula humilis* grows into a low shrubby plant with interesting thick grey-green keel-shaped leaves, usually tinged red. It has clusters of small white flowers.

*Crassula lactea* is a useful bushy species, growing up to 40cm (16in) high, with large thick leaves. This plant is particularly noted for its mass of white flowers produced in winter or early spring.

*Crassula socialis.*

*Crassula sarcocaulis.*

*Crassula* 'Silver Springtime' is especially attractive for its pyramidal rosettes of compact, very thick leaves with minute grey hairs, as well as for its white flowers.

*Crassula socialis* is a small, rosette-shaped plant which forms mats of bright green leaves. The flowers are small, but they are produced in such vast numbers that they cover the plant.

*Crassula* 'Starburst' is a fascinating little plant. It forms small columns with triangular leaves, carrying clusters of pure white flowers in the winter.

*Crassula schmidtii* is a carpeting species, with low-growing, dense rosettes of narrow leaves. It has masses of star-shaped pink flowers in the winter.

**Other good crassulas for flower:**
*Crassula falcata* has spirals of blue-grey bloomed succulent leaves which bear masses of brilliant red flowers at the apex in the late summer.

*Crassula justi-corderoyi* is a very attractive species with grey hairy leaves dotted with red and bearing pink flowers.

*Crassula* 'Morgan's Beauty' is a compact, highly succulent, grey-leaved cultivar with red flowers.

*Crassula sarcocaulis* is a fabulous tree-like plant with small leaves, which is smothered in pink flowers in the summer.

*Euphorbia milii,* the crown of thorns, is an interesting thorny euphorbia which makes a glorious show of 'flower' when its bracts, which can be red or yellow, make a mass display on the plant.

*Euphorbia milii* 'Thira' is a variegated cultivar.

Faucaria are charming small-toothed plants, which are covered in the 'curiosities' section of the next chapter but, like the lithops and other living stones, they are

*Euphorbia milii.*

*Euphorbia milii 'Thira'.*

good for flower – producing large golden yellow blooms which are surprisingly large for such small plants.

*Kalanchoe pumila* is an upright species which has particularly attractive leaves with a soft grey bloom and pretty lilac flowers. In time the weight will make it droop down, when it can be used in the same way as the trailing kalanchoes mentioned in Chapter 8.

SEDUM
Sedums are reminiscent of the crassulas in their variety of form. Good species for flower:

*Sedum cauticola* 'Lidakense' is a compact succulent, with tiny grey-green succulent leaves. It bears rich dark red flowers.

*Sedum frutescens* is an ideal miniature bonsai specimen, developing an impressive trunk and branches bearing emerald green leaves, but it is also very good for its profuse white flowers.

*Sedum pachyclados* is a mound-forming species with dark green leaves and masses of pinkish flowers.

*Sedum pluricaule* is a spreading plant, with small grey-green leaves and dark red flowers.

The two following sedum species are often grown as garden plants, when they are cut down in the winter, but they will also look good indoors.

*Sedum spectabile*, commonly known as the ice plant, has large, flat-topped pink-purple flower heads in the autumn. It grows up to 45cm (18in) and has many cultivars, which could go together into a fabulous and colourful mixed display. Look for, among others, 'Brilliant', with its bright pink heads, white-flowered 'Snow Queen' and 'Stardust', and dark purple 'Carmen' and 'Meteor'. They are easy to propagate by dividing the root stock, or by taking cuttings in the spring.

*Sedum telephium* 'Autumn Joy' has fabulous heads of purple flowers in the autumn. Leave the flowers on, because they produce attractive rust-coloured fruits in early winter, which are long-lasting and are also useful for flower arranging.

*Kalanchoe pumila.*

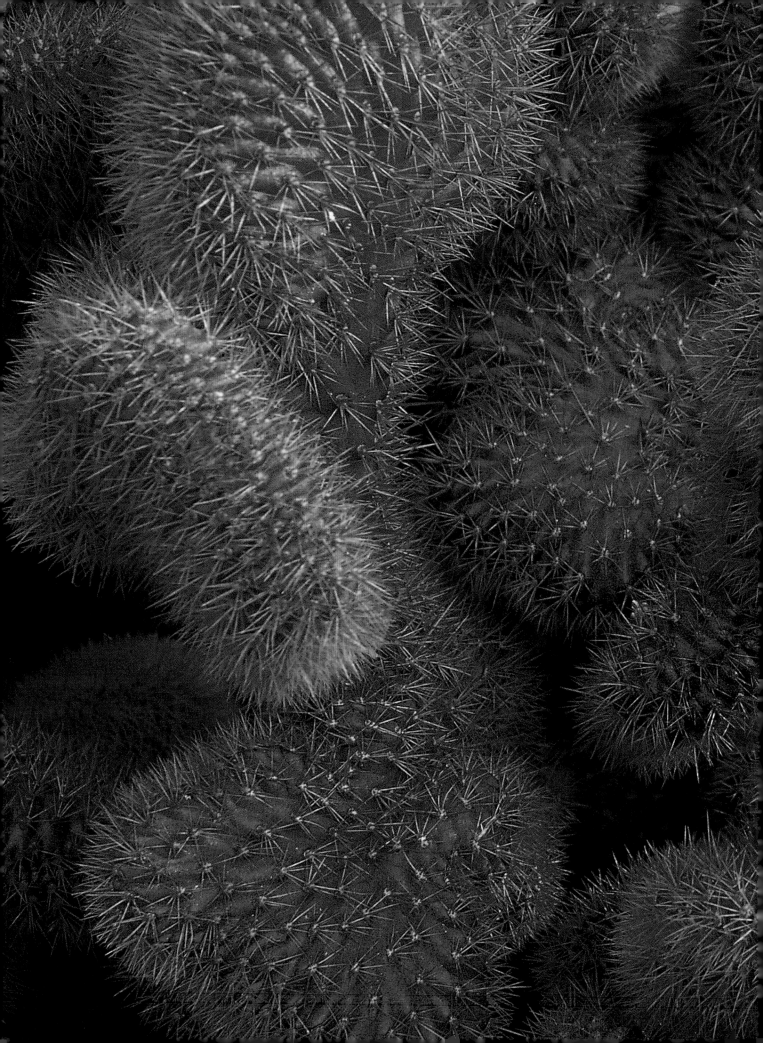

# CHAPTER 10
# FEATURE PLANTS

Bonsai-like succulents, caudiciforms, living stones, living rocks – the world of cacti and other succulents is abundant in striking curiosities

This chapter deals with particularly striking, mostly small-scale, plants. Some make fascinating miniature trees, while others deserve a bonsai-type display to show off their contorted swollen caudiciform roots or stems. Some have become so well camouflaged that they mimic living rocks or pebbles, while others have developed a leaf structure to form a mineral-like encrustation.

Many interesting species deserve to be singled out in order to show off their marvellous forms. Some cacti, for instance, have bodies which are distorted into cristate waves or strange pleats, or which carry woolly caps. Still others have fabulous markings or extraordinary spines.

These special plants are particularly good for display on a coffee table or windowsill in the house, but they can also be featured in a prominent position in your conservatory. Wherever you place them, make sure that they can be seen, because these are attention-grabbing and bizarre oddities which really do deserve to be given pride of place.

## BONSAI-TYPE OTHER SUCCULENTS

One interesting variation to consider is instant bonsai. In authentic bonsai these wonderful plants are genuine forest trees, which have been miniaturized as the result of many years of careful pruning and training.

Again, this is a wonderful hobby if you have the time or money for it, but you must either spend years growing your own or buy an expensive plant that has already been trained for you. True bonsai also have very specific care requirements in that these are hardy, outdoor trees and need careful management if they are to thrive, with long spells outside to counteract the depredation caused by time inside.

However, if you simply want the bonsai look without any purist scruples, many of the other succulents will give you easy to care for mini 'trees'. Instead of waiting 20 years (or paying a king's ransom) for the doll's house appeal of genuine miniature trees, a judicious choice of variety can give an almost immediate substitute.

## CHOOSING YOUR CONTAINER

You have to use an appropriate container if you are to create a convincing effect. The pot has to be both wide and shallow in order to give the right base to complement the spreading canopy of your 'tree'. This also has the effect of underpotting your plant, which is important as you want to restrict the growth of your subjects.

There are some really pretty bowls made especially for bonsai trees, and these come in all sorts of shapes and glazes. If you don't want to go to the trouble and expense of hunting one out, look for household crockery, like shallow flan and pie dishes, or for terracotta and glazed pottery saucers designed to sit under those giant pots at garden centres. Rectangular, square, round and oval dishes all look authentic.

A terracotta saucer planted up with *Senecio coccineiflorus*.

Bonsai-type succulents can look attractive in a landscape of stones and pebbles – but their roots must reach down into the soil.

If possible, make sure that there are drainage holes. You can drill these if they are not already present, as described earlier, but please don't forget to wear goggles or other eye protectors in case a chip flies up into your face. If you don't want to risk damaging an expensive container by drilling holes, or if you are using these containers on delicate surfaces indoors, then do avoid overwatering at all costs. Use a spray mister, or water much less frequently, and make sure the container dries out completely between waterings.

Choose a multipurpose or soil-based John Innes compost, and mix in a generous handful of horticultural grit, shingle or sharp sand. As you are starving these plants to some extent, do not add extra feed to the mix.

PLANTING UP YOUR CONTAINER
You can create either a single, specimen 'tree', a little grove or a miniforest. Choose plants with the most interesting shapes, and trim any leaves from the stems to expose the 'trunk'. You can clip the head of your tree into shape at this point, using nail scissors or pinching off pieces with your nails.

Spread the roots out into the compost. Attractive stones and pebbles can be used,

not just for landscaping but to anchor the plants while they settle into their new home. If you want a windswept look for your tree or trees, angle them to suggest this. You can also wrap bits of roots around a pebble or stone to give a gnarled effect, but do make sure the poor root eventually does end up in the soil, otherwise it will disappear like the snows of spring before you know it.

Finish the bowl with a top dressing of gravel, as well as any bits of rock or pebble that you feel are suitable. Regular trimming and pruning will keep your little trees in good shape.

SMALLER-GROWING SPECIES
(FOR MINIATURE TREES)
*Aichryson dichotomum*, also known as *A. laxum*, is a good tree-like plant reaching about 15cm (6in) in height with succulent bright green leaves growing in rosettes at the ends of the stems.

*Crassula sarcocaulis* is another excellent choice for a more miniature effect. Again, there is a distinct trunk, a branching canopy with tiny, dark green leaves and masses of pink flowers. Planted in a shallow, earthenware dish, either singly or in a little copse, they are hugely effective.

*Cotyledon orbiculata* is another miniature 'bonsai-type' tree with a superb grey bloom on the leaves. To produce really miniature leaves, starve it of water.

*Portulacaria afra*, a pretty shrub, with red, very branching stems and emerald leaves, and *P. afra* 'Follisvariegatus', with its yellow mottled leaves, can both be pruned into very convincing little trees.

*Sedum frutescens* is a particularly good choice, because the stems develop a papery bark-like skin, which peels a little like the bark on silver birches.

## LARGER-GROWING SPECIES

These high-impact, larger specimen plants will make a stunning indoors feature or an excellent focal display for a minimalist conservatory.

*Chorisia speciosa* is a rare, delightful plant with a fat spiny trunk topped with clusters of leaves. It has large yellow or red flowers and it eventually grows into a desert tree.

*Chorisia speciosa.*

*Crassula arborescens* makes a colourful and appealing bonsai specimen, with its stout succulent 'trunk' and an attractive grey bloom on green leaves with red margins. It produces pink flowers in the winter.

*Crassula ovata* (also known as *C. argentea* and *C. portulaceae*), and its attractive cultivars, mentioned above in Chapter 6 on larger plants, will in time grow into a very convincing larger tree, up to 1m (3 ft) or more tall. It has a distinctive ringed trunk, branches clothed with succulent leaves and a mass of starry flowers in the winter.

*Euphorbia atropurpurea* has succulent stems with leaves at the top. The leaves give the appearance of a miniature palm tree.

*Senecio coccineiflorus* has elongated rosettes of purple-grey leaves on a trunk-like stem and heads of scarlet flowers.

*Senecio kleinia* has thick stems bearing narrow, long leaves from near the top and can also be trained to resemble a miniature palm tree. It has grey-green bark. In its native habitat it is a freely branching shrub, reaching up to 3m (10ft), so it can be trained into a substantial specimen. (Fortunately, it is slow-growing.)

*Senecio kleinia* 'Candystick' is a variegated cultivar, with striped leaves in shades of cream and pink.

## TYLECODON

These are interesting for their gnarled shapes and for their bark. However they are very slow-growing and they are not easy to obtain.

*Tylecodon pearsonii* resembles a gnarled, branching miniature tree. It has papery, peeling greyish bark and greyish-brown long, thin succulent leaves which are shed if water is withheld, although they will regrow later. It produces pale brown flowers.

*Tylecodon reticulatus* is another 'bonsai-like' oddity, resembling an old stumpy tree. It has yellow-brown peeling bark, yellowing green flowers and long, thin yellow-green leaves, which are dropped in times of drought and later regrow.

*Tylecodon wallichii* has thick, branching stems covered with the stumps of old leaves. Again, it has peeling bark, with grey-green long, narrow, succulent leaves and yellow flowers. It eventually grows up to two metres high.

## CAUDICIFORMS

These curiosities of the plant world have a large caudex for storing water, instead of swollen leaves or stems like the true cacti and other succulents. They have a permanent water-storage organ growing at or below ground level, and this enables the

plant to survive long periods of drought. The caudex is almost inorganic in appearance, as it is always grey or brown with no hint of green. This is because chlorophyll is obtained during favourable periods, often after prolonged drought, when the plants produce ephemeral and remarkably delicate leaves and shoots, often twining and trailing in habit, which contrast very strongly with the other part of the plant. Some make interesting miniature 'trees'.

In cultivation, the storage organs are planted so that they stand above the surface of the compost to reveal their gnarled, rock-like and contorted forms. They will look particularly effective if they are displayed in the same type of 'bonsai' container which is used for your little 'trees'.

Most of these plants need a dormant period, during which they are kept almost totally dry, with just an occasional light misting to preserve the roots. They are some of the easiest plants to keep, because when the annual top growth vanishes they are telling you that their rest period is due. Start giving them more water when the top growth starts to appear again.

*Adansonia grandidieri* is the largest of all succulent plants in habitat, when it grows into a massive tree up to 30m (100ft) tall and with a trunk up to 7m (22ft) in diameter. Known as the baobab tree, it has a hugely thick trunk, reddish-grey in colour, which is quite soft, and is often taken apart by elephants. A desirable and rare novelty in any collection – and certain never to reach such giddy heights while in your care.

Caudiciform *Dioscorea elephantipes*.

*Aloinopsis jamesii.*

*Calibanus hookeri.*

*Adenia glauca* forms a large spherical caudex, from which grow tapering, climbing stems, with spiny edges and pale green leaves, and light green to yellow flowers. Can grow up to 1.5m (5ft).

*Adenia spinosa* develops a huge caudex, which can reach 2m (6ft) in diameter and 50cm (20in) high, bearing branches covered in thorns and many small leaves. It bears small yellowish-white flowers in profusion.

*Adenium obesum*, a rare and beautiful plant, is one of the showiest of all African succulents, reaching 2m (over 6ft) in habitat. It is commonly known as the desert rose or mock azalea. It has smooth, thick stems, which bear glossy green leaves and clusters of large pink flowers at their tips.

*Aloinopsis jamesii* forms an underground swollen root, bearing grey-green tapering leaves. It has golden yellow flowers with a red mid-stripe.

*Aloinopsis luckhoffii* is a small, compact plant. It has thick grey-green triangular leaves with greyish tubercles and large yellow flowers.

*Bowiea volubilis* is a good addition to a succulent collection because of its unique habit, forming a light green spherical bulb, growing above soil level, and reaching

10cm (4in) or more in diameter. It has long, thin twining stems and small greenish-white flowers.

*Bursera fagaroides* develops a gnarled swollen trunk and branches with decorative bark contrasting with the divided leaves. Highly attractive to collectors, especially lovers of bonsai.

*Calibanus hookeri* has narrow curved leaves, growing from a corky, fissured caudex.

*Cyphostemma juttae* can eventually reach 2m (6ft 6in) in height. It has a correspondingly huge caudex, an attractively peeling papery covering to its yellow bark, and thick branches which carry oval green leaves 20 x 6cm (8 x 2½in).

Cyphostemma juttae.

Ipomoea holubii.

with thick and often tuberous rhizomes, variable in appearance, many with a fleshy caudex. They usually bear masses of small flowers on a fairly long stem.

*Jatropha gossypiifolia* is a swollen-stemmed, shrubby plant reaching 2–4m (6–12ft) in habitat, with leaves divided into three lobes, red maturing to green, with distinctively red veins and edging, and bearing red flowers.

*Jatropha curcas* has a stout stem, distinctly widening at the base, and a leafy top.

*Kedrostis africana* has creeping vine-like stems reaching up to 6m (20ft) long and dark green, almost ivy-like leaves, growing from a twisted succulent caudex. It bears small green flowers.

*Nolina recurvata* has a caudex which reaches 1m (3ft) across. It produces huge, curving green leaves 1m (3ft) long from slender stems reaching 4m (12ft) upwards in habitat.

*Pelargonium carnosum*, surely a most unusual member of the geranium-type family, grows into an interesting 'miniature palm'. It has swollen, branching stems, often twisted or gnarled, up to 5cm (2in) thick. A good bonsai type of plant with numerous whitish flowers.

## IPOMOEA

Some species have an underground reservoir from which they regenerate each year, while others have greatly swollen stems: they are all rare and desirable.

*Ipomoea carnea* has tall stems, initially pear-shaped and becoming more slender towards the leafy top.

*Ipomoea holubii* has a caudex to 20cm (8in) in diameter, with thin stems produced from the top, and large deep pink to purple flowers.

## JATROPHA

These plants are related to the euphorbias, and often also have a milky sap. In their native habitat they are shrubs or small trees,

Fall guys: nine autumn-flowering living stones.

### HUNT THE LIVING STONES

Living stones, which are also known as pebble plants or mimicry plants, are all members of the family Mesembryanthemaceae.

Many people know of lithops, but there are numerous other genera to choose from, including conophytums, dinteranthus, fenestraria, frithia, gibbaeums, opthalmo-phyllums, pleiospilos and titanopsis.

Although these genera look fat and succulent, it is a mistake to think that they need a lot of water and a shady position. They originate in very arid areas and need to be treated more like true cacti, with lots of sun and just enough water. This means that they make an excellent, and curious, display for a really sunny indoor spot where no other plants can thrive. Use them by themselves or in mixed groupings in bowls, ideally with a judicious top dressing of gravel and a choice of rounded pebbles. They do look particularly attractive planted among round, glossy, polished pebbles, and can be an immensely appealing 'find the plant' amusement for little children or grandchildren – or for adults, if it comes to that.

### LITHOPS

These are the definitive living stones, which are found growing half-submerged in very dry areas of southern Africa. They have a pair of very succulent leaves, and the plant bodies strongly resemble spotted and mottled pebbles, hence their popular name. They grow by shedding their skin like a snake, with a newer, fatter and freshly invigorated plant emerging from the remnants of the dried skin of the first version. With age they form fine, many-headed clusters. Their large, daisy-like flowers, which appear from the fissured centre of the plant, are often produced when the plants are quite small. They produce their white or yellow flowers in the autumn.

There are very many to choose from: *Lithops bromfieldii* var. *insularis* 'Sulphurea' is worth hunting down, because it is a very unusual brightly coloured lime green plant with darker green mottling, lines or patches. It has yellow flowers.

*Lithops fulviceps* has a light brown to coffee-coloured body, bearing circular marks with dark orange spots and lines. It has yellow flowers.

*Lithops lesliei* is greyish-yellow to coffee, with greenish-brown spots and furrows; its flowers are golden yellow, very occasionally white.

*Lithops lesliei* 'Albinica' has a distinctly translucent, grass

Masters of disguise: lithops lend themselves to fabulous container displays which emphasize their pebble-like camouflage.

LEFT:
*Lithops salicola.*
RIGHT:
*Lithops schwantesii.*

green body, with a yellowish sheen and a yellow patterning.

*Lithops localis* forms clumps of pinkish-grey heads with dark green dots and 3cm (approximately 1in) diameter flowers.

*Lithops optica* 'Rubra', is the choicest of the lithops. It is a highly unusual, brightly-coloured, mat-forming crimson plant with brown-green patches or lines. The flowers are white and pink.

*Lithops pseudotruncatella* var. *volkii* is pale grey with distinct translucent dots.

*Lithops salicola* is grey with dotted darker grey windows and white flowers.

*Lithops schwantesii* is dark grey to orange, with bluish marks and white flowers.

CONOPHYTUM
These are popular clumping plants, many of which resemble the living stones. They, too, are autumn flowering. You could try contrasting species:

*Conophytum mundum* is a very attractive grey-green plant with raised dots and white flowers.

*Conophytum pearsonii* is bluish with mauve-pink flowers.

*Conophytum peersii* has small, clustering yellowish-green heads and cream white flowers.

*Conophytum subfenestratum* is a clump-forming species. It has a cylindrical body 2.5cm (1in) long, which is pale green with darker green spots and bears white to lilac-pink flowers.

*Conophytum ursprungianum* is an extremely beautiful species with light green heads covered in dark green dots. White flowers.

*Conphytum verrucosum* is a stone-like species, having brown stems with many grey dots.

*Conophytum subfenestratum.*

*Conophytum violaciflorum* – a clustering plant which has a dark-green body with darker spots and pretty lilac-pink flowers.

*Frithia pulchra.*

## WINDOWED LIVING STONES

Some of the lithops have partial 'windows' in the top of the leaves, with transparent sections amongst dots, lines and splotches of opaque material. However, the following species are all very distinctly windowed. In habitat they grow almost completely hidden in the soil, with only the transparent tops of the leaves peeping out, but they are grown with the leaves exposed in cultivation because they are otherwise susceptible to rotting off.

### Fenestraria

*Fenestraria aurantiaca* is a curious windowed plant with golden yellow flowers. It has the rather creepy common name of babies' toes.

*Fenestraria rhopalophylla* has transparent windows at the end of its succulent leaves to let in sunlight. White flowers.

### Frithia

These are choice stemless plants, very tiny and clustering, with distinct windows at the end of each leaf.

*Frithia pulchra* is a windowed, clump-forming mesembryanthemum with flowers of various colours, most often purple with a white centre.

*Frithia pulchra* var. *minor* is an unusual white-flowered form.

## OPHTHALMOPHYLLUM

These are living stones, again from the deserts of South Africa. They are dwarf stemless plants with two lobes, coloured green to brown or purplish. Their white, pink or lilac-red flowers are produced in autumn. These also have distinctive windows.

*Opthalmophyllum dinteri* is a dark green to coppery-red twin-lobed plant with a translucent window. It has mauvish-red flowers.

*Opthalomophyllum longum* has a greyish-green body, which can be slightly brownish below with scattered translucent dots above. The flowers go from almost white to palest pink.

*Opthalmophyllum maughanii* is a green, windowed, pebble plant bearing white daisy-like flowers in the autumn.

*Opthalmophyllum subfenestratum* is a light green plant, 2.5cm (1in) long and 1.5cm (½in or so) across. It has two rounded lobes with translucent dots, and 2cm (⅞in) diameter white and pink flowers.

*Opthalmophyllum vanheerdei* is reddish brown with a translucent window and white to pale pink flowers.

*Opthalmophyllum spathulatum* is a solitary dark green or brown, windowed, pebble plant with pale pink flowers.

## GIBBAEUM

These plants are also two-lobed, but rather larger than the species described above. They

Titanopsis.

are also distinctly lopsided, with one lobe always larger than the other, often to a really marked degree.

*Gibbaeum comptonii* consists of two rounded thick lobes, bluish-green in colour and forming mats a few centimetres high. The plants have pinkish-purple flowers.

*Gibbaeum heathi* is a fissured spherical whitish-green plant, 2–3cm (about 1 in) across and high. White or pink flowers.

*Gibbaeum dispar* has two unequal, roughly egg-shaped leaves with a greyish-green surface. This clump-forming species has mauve flowers.

### PLEIOSPILOS

This is another mimicry genus, with pairs of very thick leaves similar to lithops, some having a granite-like pebbly appearance, while others produce longer, more pointed and succulent leaves. They can form large clumps with time and are very popular for their freely produced autumn flowers in a variety of colours.

*Pleiospilos bolusii* is remarkable for producing large golden flowers from plants which look like two pieces of grey rock.

*Pleiospilos magnipunctatus* is a readily clumping species, producing pale lemon flowers from between the thick grey leaves.

*Pleiospilos nelii* is grey-green and almost spherical, with salmon pink flowers.

*Pleisospilos peersii* has very succulent grey-green leaves, and yellow flowers which have a white centre.

### TITANOPSIS

This is another really interesting genus, in which the mimicry is taken to even greater heights. The plants have encrusted leaves, with a greyish-white textured finish, to camouflage them amongst the glittering quartz rocks of their habitat.

*Titanopsis fulleri* has rock-like, bluish-green leaves on short stems, forming mats. It has dark yellow flowers.

*Titanopsis calcarea* has encrusted blue-grey leaves and golden yellow flowers.

*Titanopsis luederitzii* has grey leaves with 'rocky' areas at the tips and yellow flowers.

*Schwantesia herrei* is similar to the titanopsis with its encrusted, stony appearance.

## OTHER ODDITIES

### LIVING ROCKS

Ariocarpus is a fascinating genus of cacti. Its members look just like rocks, with tubercles producing knobbly outgrowths and fissures. In their natural habitat they grow almost fully submerged, with only their top surface visible, but they are grown in more exposed conditions in cultivation.

Again, this is a safety precaution as much as a matter of aesthetics, because it is much easier to keep an eye on their condition if you can see them. They are very slow-growing, with a hugely thickened root, but they are rewarding, producing attractive flowers with time.

*Ariocarpus fissuratus* has large grey tubercles with a fissured and uneven surface. It is slow-growing, but clumps with age, when it also produces beautiful pink flowers.

*Ariocarpus kotschoubeyanus* has purple flowers which are readily produced.

*A. kotschoubeyanus* var. *albiflora* is the white-flowered version of this rare and slow-growing plant.

*Ariocarpus retusus* develops a large tap-root and grey tubercles, and has cream flowers.

*Ariocarpus retusus* var. *furfuraceus* has triangular, pointed tubercles forming a glaucous green mosaic. It has white flowers.

*Ariocarpus trigonus* has large grey tubercles shaped into a crown, and yellow flowers.

## UNUSUAL CACTI

Cacti and succulents also offer interesting possibilities for smaller, feature planting where your oddities and curiosities are prominently displayed, and where their small-scale but interesting features can be seen and appreciated. This makes them a perfect choice as houseplants.

*Aztekium ritteri* is a unique, very choice, plant, spineless except when very young. It is a wrinkly ribbed species which has a distinctive flattened globular and creased appearance. A slowgrowing species, it will eventually offset to form a small clump. Its flowers are white or pink. It is more demanding than most cacti, as it needs both higher temperatures and better drainage.

### ASTROPHYTUM
This is a very recognizable genus, which has attracted a number of common names because the bodies are so very distinctive.

*Astrophytum asterias*, or the sea urchin cactus, is a very attractive plant. Spherical and spineless, with a greyish body, patterned with white dots, it does genuinely look like the sea creature. The large yellow flowers are red-centred, making this one of the choicest members of the group.

*Astrophytum capricorne*, the goat horn cactus, has a superb, white-speckled body, with a tangle of long, twisted spines. It has large yellow flowers.

*Astrophytum capricorne* var. *major* is like the above, but bigger everywhere.

*Astrophytum asterias* hybrid.

*Astrophytum ornatum.*

*Astrophytum myriostigma* is called the bishop's cap cactus, because it is completely spineless and its five angular ribs give it its suggestion of distinctive clerical headgear. A very attractive greyish plant, it is closely spotted with white and has large yellow flowers.

*Astrophytum ornatum*, with its curved spines, body strongly speckled with white dots and light yellow flowers, is another very good-looking plant.

*Astrophytum senile* is another appealing species with long, curving grey and black spines, and large yellow flowers.

### BLOSSFELDIA

These are miniature gems, the smallest of all cacti. They are globular in shape, spineless and clumping with age. They have minute white or pink flowers.

*Blossfeldia liliputana* is a very small greyish-green plant, growing only to about 1cm (³⁄₈in) in diameter.

*Blossfeldia liliputana* var. *fechseri* is glossy green, its delicate white translucent flowers having rounded petals.

*Blossfeldia pedicellata* is a rare member of the genus. Slow-growing but worth a try. It has tiny white flowers.

### COPIAPOA

These plants deserve a place on the strength of their colour, which makes them one of the most interesting groups of spherical cacti. They vary from floury white through grey-green to dark-brown/black, and most species have perfumed yellow flowers.

*Copiapoa cinerea* var. *haseltoniana* grows into a dramatic large globular plant with a chalky grey skin and black spines. Yellow flowers.

*Copiapoa humilis* is small, spherical and deep green to olive green, sometimes with a reddish overlay. Bristly with fine white spines and a longer central spine, and bearing yellow flowers.

*Copiapoa hypogaea* is a fabulous, very dramatic black plant with black spines and contrasting yellow flowers tinged pink.

*Copiapoa pendulina* is a strongly spined greyish-red species with yellow flowers.

*Copiapoa tenuissima* is a striking olive green, with grey spines and yellowish-pink flowers.

*Copiapoa humilis.*

## DISCOCACTUS

All of the plants in this genus are rare and much sought-after for their large nocturnal flowers borne on a cephalium, a woolly or bristly crown at the top of the plant from where the flowers originate. They are also prized for their strongly textured bodies, which have pronounced ribs or prominent warty tubercles. The plants do, however, need a minimum winter temperature of 10°C (50°F), so they are a choice for the house or heated conservatory.

*Discocactus horstii* is smallest of this species, to about 1cm (under ½in). Its dark purplish-brown body has narrow ribs with tiny clusters of spider-like spines.

*Discocactus placentiformis* is another choice species, olive green with thick, short, curved spines and large white flowers.

## ECHINOFOSSULOCACTUS

This genus (also known as stenocactus) has an interesting, much-crinkled and wavy, ribbed habit, appearing almost artificially pleated, often with very strong spination.

*Echinofossulocactus albatus* is bluish-green, with curious wavy ribs and pure white flowers.

*Echinofossulocactus crispatus* grows quite quickly for this genus; it has numerous, narrow, wavy ribs and purple flowers.

*Echinofossulocactus hastatus* is dark green with many wavy, narrow ribs and strong spines. It has white and pink flowers.

*Echinofossulocactus heteracanthus* is strikingly corrugated, as it has 40 to 50 thin wavy, closely pleated ribs. It bears greenish-yellow flowers.

*Echinofossulocactus phyllacanthus* is a round, white-spined plant with numerous wavy ribs and abundant cream and brown flowers.

*Echinofossulocactus tricuspidatus* has up to 55 wavy ribs and yellow-green flowers.

*Hilderwinteria aureispinus* is an interesting, sprawling cactus with branching pendant stems and producing orange-pink flowers which last for several days and nights.

*Leuchtenbergia principis* is a literally unique species as it is the only member of this genus. It grows as an angular rosette, with upright, hugely elongated blue-grey tubercles and long, soft, white raffia-like spines. It has large silken yellow flowers which grow from a tubercle at the apex of the plant.

LEFT: *Echinofossulocactus crispatus*.
RIGHT: *E. tricuspidatus*.

Cristate form of euphorbia species.

## CRISTATE AND MONSTROUS FORMS

These plants are worth a section of their own, as they are strange, almost grotesque deformities which nevertheless exercise a strange fascination. Genetic factors, damage to the growing point or a virus infection are suspected as possible causes of these mutations. To keep them looking good – or, perhaps I should say, looking bad – you need constantly to remove any normal growth, or the plant will revert back to being its virtuous, rather than its evil, twin.

*Cereus jamacaru* var. *monstrosus* is a fabulous, glossy green monster.

*Cereus peruvianus* var. *monstrosus* is a glossy blue-green sculptured work of art.

*Opuntia robusta* var. *monstrosus* grows into attractive miniature grey columns with very small elongated pads.

*Opuntia tuna* var. *monstrosus* has clustering small, bright green pads on flattened elongated stems.

*Opuntia vestita* var. *cristata* forms prickly, densely hairy undulating forms.

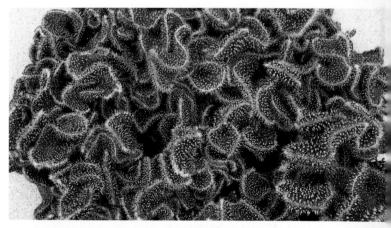

TOP TO BOTTOM: Cristate forms of *Bolivicereus samaipetanus*, echinopsis species, *Opuntia cylindrica* and lobivia species.

## CRISTATE MAMMILLARIA
These densely spined waves of undulating yellow or white are stupendous.

*Mammillaria elongata* var. *cristata* is a beautiful cristate form of the golden-spined species.

*Mammillaria lanata* var. *cristata* forms twisting waves covered in short white spines and bearing red flowers.

*Mammillaria zeilmanniana* var. *cristata* is a rare cristate form of this popular species. It grows in curving waves rather than in the usual globular form.

## MELOCACTUS
These are also much prized for the cephaliums they produce, which are so prominent and markedly cylindrical that the genus is known by the common name, Turk's cap. They are also tender, like the discocactus, and need winter temperatures of 10°C (50°F) so, again, they should be kept indoors or in a heated conservatory.

*Melocactus azureus* is an attractive blue, even when young, becoming more intensely coloured with age. It eventually forms a pineapple-size cephalium.

*Melocactus matanzanus* will, at a relatively small size, form a creamy-white woolly cephalium suffused with gingery spines.

*Melocactus neryi* is a choice, dark green plant up to 11cm (4in) tall and a little broader. Carmine flowers are carried on older plants.

*Melocactus onchyacanthus* is an attractive species to grow while you wait for it to reach the 12cm (5–6in) diameter at which the cephalium forms, because the body of the plant is enveloped by thick, curling spines.

*Melocactus salvadorensis* with age develops a crest, or cephalium, of wool and bristles from which the numerous, small pink flowers emerge.

*Melocactus violaceus* is small-growing, and forms a white cephalium set off by dark brown spines. Tiny deep pink to purple flowers.

## PECTINATE CACTUS
These genera are much prized for their **pectinate** spines. They have a densely packed, feathery appearance, like the teeth of a comb, and are almost artificial in their perfect symmetry, which makes them both distinctive and desirable.

*Pelecyphora* (also known as *Strombocactus*) *pseudopectinatus* var. *rubriflora* is a rare and prized plant which initially has globular stems, later elongating, with numerous short, feathery spines and red flowers.

*Pelecyphora* (*Strombocactus*) *valdezianus* is a miniature rarity with hair-like, feathery spines and violet, pink flowers.

*Pelecyphora* (*Strombocactus*) *valedezianus* var. *albiflora* is the white-flowered variety.

*Solisia pectinata* is a slow growing rarity with dense, white comb-like spines and pink flowers.

*Pelcyphora asselliformis, a pectinate cactus.*

LEFT: *Turbinicarpus schmiedickeanus var. macrochele*.
RIGHT: *Chasmatophyllum muscolinum*.

## TURBINICARPUS

These are choice, small-growing plants with blue-green or grey-green stems and papery, curved spines. They are covetable little gems, which also have the bonus of producing relatively large flowers for such tiny plants.

*Turbinicarpus schmiedickeanus* var. *dicksoniae* has cream flowers with a darker mid-stripe.

*Turbinicarpus laui* is a rare species with white 'feathery' spines.

*Turbinicarpus lophophoroides* is grey, its white flowers tinged a delicate pink.

*Turbinicarpus pseudomacrochele* has bristly, flexible, interlacing spines, yellow at first but later grey. White flowers with pink mid-stripe.

*Turbinocarpus schmiedickeanus* is a choice miniature, up to 2.5cm (1in) across and covered in broad papery spines. It has white or pink flowers.

*Turbinicarpus schmiedickeanus* var. *flaviflorus* has yellow flowers, masses of white wool and soft, curving spines.

*Turbinicarpus schmiedickeanus* var. *gracilis* is a grey-green plant with cream flowers having a pinkish mid-stripe on each petal.

*Turbinicarpus schmiedickeanus* var. *klinkerianus* is an attractive grey plant with cream flowers which are regularly produced in the spring.

*Turbinicarpus schmiedickeanus* var. *macrochele* is a good-looking plant with tangled spines and white flowers, suffused with pink. The spines are long and grey, curving inwards like flat, flexible hooks.

*Turbinicarpus schmiedickeanus* var. *schwarzii* is a grey-green plant, its cream flowers having a pale pink central stripe on each petal. It has soft, grey, curved spines, very few in number.

## UNUSUAL SUCCULENTS

*Chasmatophyllum muscolinum* has small, thick, grey knobbly-toothed leaves forming a mat of short-stemmed plants. Yellow flowers.

*Cheiridopsis peculiaris* is a small-growing plant with succulent grey-green leaves and yellow flowers.

*Euphorbia obesa*, or Hottentot's hut, to give its rather non-pc name, is a peculiar plant. It is almost freakishly spherical and spineless, and develops strongly marked grey, green and red stripes with age. The patterning is so strong that it can almost appear like tartan. This species has insignificant yellow flowers.

Not to be sniffed at: *Stapelia flavopurpurea* is good on the eye, but its flowers carry the stench of death.

## STAPELIA

These plants are interesting for two rather opposing qualities. The flowers are truly spectacular, huge and fleshy, often shaped like fat starfish and coloured in maroon, beige, yellow and brown, with blotched and splashed markings. So far so good. The plants are indeed striking, both as thickened succulent plants, with a variety of finger-like forms, and when in flower. Unfortunately the smell of the flowers is far from fragrant: as they are pollinated by flies that are tricked into seeing the blooms as carrion, they carry the pungent odour of death. This is, therefore, definitely not one for the house when in flower. Some species are undergoing changes of name, but the following are in common use:

*Stapelia ambigua* has huge star-shaped hairy flowers.
*Stapelia arnotii* has flowers 10cm (4in) across in shades of dark red.
*Stapelia asterias* var. *lucida* has glossy purple-brown flowers.
*Stapelia flavirostris* is a vigorous plant which has very large, purple, star-shaped, hairy flowers with wavy yellow lines.
*Stapelia flavopurpurea* has yellow and red flowers.
*Stapelia gemmiflora* has remarkable black flowers.

*Stapelia gettleffii* has velvety, clumping, angled stems with purple, yellow and white flowers.
*Stapelia gigantea* has huge red and yellow flowers.
*Stapelia leendertziae* produces dark purple flowers.
*Stapelia margarita* (also know as *S. hirsuta*) has dramatic, star-shaped flowers, dull red with yellowish wrinkles, and a dense cushion of reddish hairs.
*Stapelia namaquensis* var. *ciliolata* carries yellow and purple flowers.
*Stapelia nobilis* has slightly hairy, four-angled stems, bearing dark red and yellow flowers which are 20–25cm (8–10in) across.
*Stapelia revoluta* var. *tigrida* has reddish flowers with a green star in the centre.
*Stapelia revoluta* has greenish-yellow flowers.
*Stapelia schinzii* has clusters of tall, thin angular stems bearing huge black star-shaped flowers.
*Stapelia trifida* has large yellow and purple flowers.
*Stapelia variegata* has beautiful star-shaped yellow and purple flowers which have to be seen to be believed.
*Stapelia verrucosa* has clumping, angled, brown and green stems with yellow, red and brown flowers.
*Stapelia youngii* has large yellow and purple flowers.

See also *Diplocyatha ciliata*, a mat-forming greyish-broze plant with 7–8cm (3in) diameter creamy-white flowers.

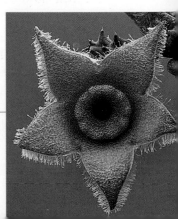

Heavenly: the lovely star-shaped flower of *Diplocyatha ciliata*.

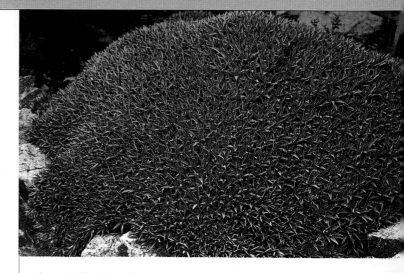

Abromeitiella chlorantha.

FAUCARIA (TIGERS' JAWS)

Faucaria are all interesting miniature succulent plants, with markedly toothed leaf edges which look like the mouths of ferocious, if tiny, green animals! They have the bonus of producing large, golden yellow flowers.

*Faucaria albidens* has triangular, tapering leaves, horny on the top surface, and golden yellow flowers.

*Faucaria bosscheana* has thick, crowded, succulent keel-shaped leaves with a lighter edge and golden yellow flowers.

*Faucaria britteniae* has thick, succulent green stems and large yellow flowers.

*Faucaria candida* has large white flowers, very unusual for this genus.

*Faucaria felina* has tapering leaves, green to reddish, with pointed tubercles on the edges and the usual golden yellow flowers.

*Faucaria gratiae* branches to form a mat of thick, fleshy, toothed leaves starred with large golden yellow flowers.

*Faucaria kingiae* has bluish-green leaves, becoming dotted with white in older plants.

*Faucaria longidens* has large yellow flowers with a white centre.

*Faucaria longifolia* has long, narrow, grey-green leaves and large, dark yellow flowers.

*Faucaria lupina* has long, triangularly tapering leaves, fresh green, with tiny rough dots, and toothed. It has the usual yellow flowers.

*Faucaria paucidens* has yellow flowers.

*Faucaria subintegra* has thick grey-green leaves and yellow flowers.

*Faucaria tigrina* is the eponymous tiger's jaws, with yellow flowers.

*Faucaria tuberculosa* has thick triangular-shaped leaves with tubercles and teeth, and the usual large yellow flowers.

And last, but not least, these fierce looking specimens:

*Abromeitiella chlorantha* forms huge mounds of small rosettes, consisting of small triangular leaves, tipped with a spine. It has yellow flowers 2cm (⁷⁄₈in) long.

*Abromeitiella lorentziana* forms a grey-green mass which can reach 1m (3ft) across, and which is made up of rosettes of spiky, triangular leaves 4–15cm (1½–6in) long, with toothed margins and a terminal spine. It has greenish flowers.

Faucaria tigrina.

# Glossary

**Accent planting** – a particularly large and dramatic plant or plants, used as the most important feature in a scheme

**Acid soil** – soil that has a pH value of less than 7

**Architectural** – plants that have a particularly strong shape and form

**Areole** – of cacti, the portion of the plant from which the spines originate

**Basal caudex** – see caudex

**Bi-colours** – leaves or flowers that have two contrasting shades

**Bloom (or felt)** – blue or greyish fine, waxy or powdery coating on leaves or stems

**Bonsai** – system, originating in Japan, of miniaturisation of trees by restriction of roots and pruning of top growth

**Bonsai-like succulents** – tree-like succulents, which make instant or almost instant miniature trees for growing in pots

**Borrowed heat** – heat which escapes from intentionally warmed spaces into unheated adjacent spaces; e.g. an unheated conservatory, which will remain warmer than a freestanding structure because heat escapes into it through the house walls

**Botanical nomenclature** – international system of classification of plants into families, genera and species

**Bract** – a modified leaf, often large and brightly coloured, which is produced at the base of a flower or a flower cluster

**Cachepots** – decorative pots without drainage holes: they act as sleeves for normal plastic pots and protect interior surfaces from water damage while looking attractive

**Cactus (cacti)** – a member of the Cactaceae family, usually highly succulent, with spines produced from areoles

**Candelabrum (of plants)** – a plant with a number of branching arms

**Caudex** – swollen base of stem or root of a succulent plant, adapted as a water-storage organ

**Caudiciform** – a plant which forms a caudex

**Cephalium** – densely spined, woolly cap at the top of a cactus stem, from which flowers are produced

**Chamfering (of grafting)** – making angled cuts to the edes of the scion and the stock so that they fit together well, to improve the chance of a successful graft taking

**Chlorophyll** – the green pigment in plant leaves and stems which absorbs energy from sunlight

**CITES** – the Convention on International Trade in Endangered Species of Wild Fauna and Flora. These regulations have been designed to prohibit the removal of endangered species from their natural habitat, and to control the trade in these species. The members of the family cactaceae involved are listed in Appendix 1 of CITES

**Cleft graft** – see grafting, scion, stock: a form of graft designed for relatively flat scions, in which the scion is inserted and fastened down into a central slit which has been cut into the surface of the stock

**Columnar** – with an upright habit of growth, forming tall, cylindrical structures

**Cristate** – a deformed plant, where the growing point has developed an abnormal crested or twisted form

**Cultivar** – an artificially produced plant, either bred or selected, which can be propagated while retaining its characteristics.

**Cylindrical (of plants)** – see columnar

**Debud/disbud** – remove buds to prevent flowering

**Desiccated** – dehydrated and dried up

**Diagonal graft** – see grafting, scion, stock: a form of graft designed for slender scions, in which the surfaces of the scion and the stock are joined with slanting, diagonal cuts to give the maximum area of contact between them

**Diurnal** – of a flower, opening during the day

**Dormancy** – a period of low or absent plant growth, usually associated with low winter temperatures and light levels

**Drought resistant** – able to tolerate periods without water

**Elliptical** – with the shape of a flattened circle, like a rugby ball

**Epiphytic cacti** – pendant cacti which, in habitat, root in the moist debris in tree branches

**Ericaceous (of compost)** – acidic, and therefore suitable for acid-loving plants

**Etiolated** – grown tall, spindly and pale because of too little light

**Evergreen** – with leaves all the year round: although leaves do die and are replaced, this is a continuous process and therefore unnoticeable

**Felt** – see bloom

**Filigree-like** – of a delicate, interlacing habit, resembling the fine, lace-like patterns in twisted silver and gold jewellery

**Flat grafting** – see grafting, scion, stock: the 'normal' form of graft, where the scion and stock are joined together at horizontally cut surfaces

**Focal planting** – the most visually important plants in a scheme, placed to draw the greatest possible attention

**Frost hardy** – see hardy

**Fully hardy** – see hardy

**Fungicide** – a chemical formulated to treat fungal (non-photosynthesizing, mould-like) plant infections

**Genus (genera)** – a group of species which share enough common characteristics to be grouped together for the purpose of botanical identification

**Globular** (of plants) – having a spherical or ball-like shape

**Glochids** – bristles or barbed hairs carried on the areoles of cacti

**Grafting** – a method of propagation by which a rare, slow-growing or difficult-to-cultivate plant is removed from its own roots (thus becoming the scion) and artificially attached to a more vigorous, rooted parent plant (the stock)

**Ground cover** – carpeting and mat-forming species that rapidly cover bare areas

**Habitat** – original geographical area where the plants grow wild

**Half-hardy** – plants which can only go outside after any danger of frost has passed and which have to come indoors for the winter before frosts are likely

**Hard core** – material, such as broken bricks and rocks, which acts as a compacted foundation layer for a surface material like gravel or paving slabs

**Hardy** – describes the resilience of plant to cold, subdivided into frost hardy: able to withstand temperatures down to -5°C (23°F); and fully hardy: able to withstand temperatures to -15°C (5°F)

**High maintenance** – a scheme that will demand a great deal of time and attention

**Hybrid** – offspring of at least two different species or varieties or plant, which can be naturally or artificially produced

**In-filling** – temporary planting to fill in a bed or border until the permanent planting matures sufficiently to fill the space

**Inflorescence** – a flowering shoot which carries more than one flower

**Insecticide** – a toxic substance for destroying insect pests

**Low maintenance** – easy-care planting schemes requiring the minimum of attention

**Mealy bug** – major pest of cacti and other succulents, characterized by a white, woolly appearance. Found as leaf and root mealy bugs

**Mid-stripe** – a central band of contrasting colour in a leaf or flower petal

**Non-invasive** – a plant that will not outgrow its position or affect neighbouring plants

**Offsetting** – a plant which produces miniature replicas of itself, usually around its base

**Panicles** – a branched flower cluster

**Papilla** (plural **papillae**) – soft and small wart-like outgrowths

**Papillose** – covered in minute, blunt projections

**Pectinate** – comb-like

**Plumes** – feather-like heads

**Pricking out** – transplanting seedlings or young plants which are becoming crowded into another container to give them more space to grow

**Propagating** – producing extra plants by setting seeds, taking cuttings, grafting etc

**Propagator** – a container, with heat and/or light, which gives seeds, cuttings etc the best possible conditions for maximum growth

**Prostrate** – a sprawling, low-growing habit

**Racemes** – unbranched flower clusters

**Red spider mite** – minute, fast-moving pest which must be treated quickly, as it spreads rapidly

**Ribs** – a feature of some cacti, which have their surface divided into raised sections bearing areoles

**Rosette-shaped/forming** (of leaves) – radiating from a central point

**Rule of 3 or 5** – the fact that irregular numbers of plants of the same species create a more natural look, by blending irregularly into adjacent planting

**Scale insect** – pest which clings, limpet-like, to the surface of a plant

**Sciarid fly** – pest of damp, peat-based composts, which removes dead vegetable matter but is lethal to the tiny roots of seedlings

**Scion** – see grafting, stock, vascular tissue: the part of a rare, slow-growing or difficult-to-cultivate plant which has been removed from its own roots and artificially attached to a more vigorous-rooted parent plant

**Species** – a member of a genus

**Spines/spination** – a hard outgrowth from a stem: in cacti they are an evolutionary modification of leaves

**Staging** – a system of shelving for the display and maintenance of plants

**Stock** – see grafting, scion, vascular tissue: a vigorous plant, with its top section removed to be replaced by an artificially attached rootless section of a rare, slow-growing or difficult-to-cultivate plant, which will grow more successfully with the support of the host plant's root sytem

**Strata** – the distinct layers laid down during the formation of sedimentary rock

**Subspecies** – members of a species which share common features within themselves

**Succulent (succulence)** – a plant that has evolved to withstand periods of drought, by modifying the leaves, stems or roots for improved water storage

**Syrphid fly** – natural predator for controlling mealy bug pest

**Systemic insecticide** – a longer-lasting chemical taken up into the whole of the plant so that it continues to poison insects which feed on it; as opposed to a non-systemic insecticide, which coats the outside of the plant and insects temporarily but is soon washed away

**Terminal spines** – spines at the extreme end of a leaf, shoot, stem or other plant structure

**Trailing** – a plant with long stems which hang down, particularly useful for baskets, window boxes etc

**Transpiration** – evaporation of water from plants via the stems and leaves

**Tubercles** – small, warty protuberances

**Umbel** – a flat or rounded inflorescence, which has a number of flowers on individual stalks growing from a single terminal point

**Underpotting** – deliberately using a too-small pot for one of a number of reasons: to restrict the growth of a plant, to trigger flower production or simply because the plant thrives in confined conditions

**Variegation** – foliage that displays lighter banding, striping or spotting

**Vascular tissue** – a slightly darker core in the centre of a stem, surrounded by a circle of cells which act as water-storing tissue. For a graft to be successful, the vascular tissue in both the stock and scion has to be in contact in at least one place

**Vegetative propagation** – the increase of plants by cuttings, grafts or removing offsets, as opposed to raising plants from seed

**Vestigial** – simple in structure, with reduced size and function

**Zygomorphic** – producing flowers which are symmetrical in only one plane, as in a Christmas cactus bloom, as opposed to producing flowers with the more usual radial symmetry, as seen in the spokes of a wheel.

# Further reading

I hope that this book has interested and entertained you, and that you have been inspired to give some space in your house or conservatory to these easy-going, good-looking and fascinating plants.

However, there is much, much more out there! The whole area of cacti and the other succulents is vast, and in a book of this length it is impossible to cover more than a fraction of the genera which are available. If you want to expand your interest, the care, propagation and display guidelines explained in the preceding chapters apply for most succulent plants, apart from a very few of the most challenging and exotic rarities.

Don't feel, therefore, that you are tied to the genera and species which I have described, as there are many more fine plants to discover. In the further reading list which follows I have listed photographic encyclopaedias dedicated to true cacti and to the other succulents, which will give you plenty of inspiration. There are also more specific books should you fall in love with, say, aloes or the living stones.

If you would like to learn more about this complex and fascinating world of plants, the following are good sources to begin with.

*Cacti and Succulents, Step by Step to Growing Success*, Bill Keen, Crowood Gardening Guide, 1999 (first published 1990)
An excellent, readable book for a newcomer to the plants, and one of the best we've ever seen about looking after these subjects. It covers care, propagation, and pests and diseases, and sets out a good selecton of suitable plants. Comprehensive and well illustrated.

*Cacti, the Illustrated Dictionary*, Rod and Ken Preston-Mafham, Cassell 1998 (first published 1991 by Blandford)
A huge photographic guide to the globular cacti, over 1,000 species presented in colour photographs, alphabetically arranged, along with brief descriptions of the plants and invaluable details of alternative names.

*Glossary of Botanical Terms with special reference to Succulent Plants*, compiled by Urs Eggli, British Cactus and Succulent Society, 1993
A really useful alphabetical dictionary of botanical terms with several pages of line drawings explaining terms for leaf and flower shapes, etc.

*Guide to the Aloes of South Africa*, Ben-Erik Van Wyk and Gideon Smith, Briza, 1996
With more than 400 colour photographs, showing plants in habitat and close-ups of leaves and flowers, this book features plant descriptions of the 125 species of the region, split into groups based on habit of growth and with helpful distribution maps. It also deals with related aloe-like plants, such as agaves and gasterias; medicinal and cosmetic uses; and conservation issues.

*The Cactus Handbook*, Tony Sato, Japan Cactus Planning Press, 1996
This is a wonderful picture book for the enthusiast, an excellent plant identifier, written in Japanese and English with botanical names under each colour photograph. 345 pages and more than 3,000 excellent colour photographs.

*Lithops – Treasures of The Veld*, Steven Hammer, British Cactus & Succulent Society, 1999
Softback 148 pages; 225 colour photographs, 10 line drawing and 2 maps

*Mesembryanthemums Of The World, an Illustrated Guide to a Remarkable Succulent Group*, (multiple authorship), Briza, 1998
A hard-back book, 405 pages, lavishly illustrated with more than 800 colour photographs

*Succulents, the Illustrated Dictionary*, Maurizio Sajeva and Mariangela Constanzo, Cassell, 1994 (last reprint 1998).
This is the companion volume to the Preston-Mafham *Cacti, the Illustrated Dictionary*, but dealing with the 'other' succulents. Includes more than 1,200 photographs of species and varieties from 195 different genera.

*Succulents II, the Illustrated Dictionary*, Maurizio Sajeva and Mariangela Costanzo, Timber Press, 2000
This has the same layout as *Succulents*, above, with more than 1,200 colour photographs and including more than 900 species not illustrated in the first book. Every species illustrated is described with information on shape, size, colour and growth form, plus country of origin and CITES status. Introductory chapters cover habitat and genera information plus cultivation details.

**The following are out of print but worth looking out for in libraries or second-hand bookshops:**

*Cacti for the Connoisseur*, John Pilbeam, B T Batsford, 1987
The book for a definitive list of currently accepted names – there have been many changes over the years.

*The Cactus Handbook*, Erik Haustein, Cathay Books, 1988
An encyclopaedia covering columnar as well as globular cacti, but most useful for its readable introduction to all the botany you would ever need to know for cactus collecting.

*The Illustrated Encyclopaedia of Cacti*, Clive Innes and Charles Glass, Headline, 1991
Illustrates and identifies over 1,200 species, including columnar and epiphytic cacti as well as just the globular species.

*The Illustrated Encyclopaedia of Succulents*, Gordon Rowley, Salamander Books, 1978
Crammed full of pictures, it includes both cacti and succulents, and the author has a wonderfully anecdotal style.

# Further information

As with any hobby, you will find that there are many sources of information – specialist societies, journals, websites and so on – to add to your knowledge:

BRITISH CACTUS AND
SUCCULENT SOCIETY
The objectives of the society are to promote the study, conservation, propagation and cultivation of cacti and other succulent plants.

Membership of the BCSS (open to all) is currently about 3,800, and includes the whole range from novice windowsill growers to experts. The society has just under a hundred branches in the UK. As well as holding local meetings and shows, and producing an information-packed quarterly magazine, the society has 'round robin' groups on a number of topics. Group members share ideas and information.

Membership secretary:
D V Slade, 15 Brentwood Crescent,
Hull Road, York, Y010 5HU (01904 410512)

THE CACTUS AND SUCCULENT
PLANT MALL
Website: http://www.cactus-mall.com
An internet resource for all growers of cacti and succulent plants, this is regularly updated with information on cactus and succulent societies and suppliers of plants, seeds and literature on cacti and succulents. The CSPM has developed, and hosts, webpages for more than a hundred organizations worldwide. It also aims to maintain as complete a list of web pages and other cactus- and succulent-related Internet facilities as possible. The Mall includes the official webpages for the world's three largest cactus and succulent societies.

THE AMATEURS' DIGEST
Edited by Marina Welham, this is a bi-monthly publication written and illustrated by lovers of succulent plants. A friendly and helpful publication, it has a welcoming manner and is packed with interesting features.

Information from and subscriptions to:
Marina Welham, The Amateurs' Digest,
Department G, 8591 Lochside Drive,
Sidney, BC, V8L IM5, Canada

The Amateurs' Digest has a comprehensive, friendly and informative website
www.TheAmateursDigest.com
E-mail address: amatrdigest@coastnet.com

SOFTWARE
*The Lexicon of Cacti Names, millennium edition, 2000*
A computer software package, based on recent literature and compiled by Lucio and Vittoria Mondolfo, to collate information on legitimate cactus names, and also to list their synonyms. Has the benefit of ease of use, good search facilities and regular updates.

Available from Mike Whitlock, Cactusbase, 38 Alexandra Road, Rayleigh, Essex SS6 8HS, UK. E-mail: enquiries@cactusbase.com; website: www.cactusbase.com

# About the author

Since 1977 Shirley-Anne Bell has been building up her own retail and mail-order plant business in Lincolnshire, England, with the assistance of her photographer husband, Neville.

While raising their three children, Shirley-Anne gained a first-class honours degree with the Open University in History of Art, Architecture and Design, and English. During the 1980s her poetry was widely published and she was a writer in residence, ran writing workshops, gave national readings, was a literature consultant for Lincolnshire and Humberside Arts, and edited *Proof*, the regional literary magazine.

Shirley-Anne's first cacti book, *Growing Cacti and Other Succulents in the Garden,* was also published by GMC, and she is a regular contributor to GMC's *Exotic Gardening* magazine. The nursery publishes its own catalogues and guides and has a vast picture library, including photographs taken on travels overseas.

To speak to Shirley-Anne and for more information contact:
Glenhirst Cactus Nursery, Station Road, Swineshead, near Boston, Lincolnshire PE20 3NX. Tel: 01205 820314, fax: 01205 820614, e-mail: sabell@glenhirstcactiandpalms.co.uk
website: www.glenhirstcactiandpalms.co.uk

# Index

# Acknowledgements

GENERAL ACKNOWLEDGEMENTS

I would like to thank Neville for all of the photography in the book, and for unflaggingly continuing to add extra material right up to the last moment – and also for his hard work on producing so many beautiful and spick and span plants, and for his encouragement and input at every stage of writing the book, from first drafts to final, final, final ones. I would also like to thank him, plus my mum and our son Jon, for helping to keep the business running smoothly even when I wasn't.

Special thanks must go to my good-natured and eagle-eyed editor, David Arscott, who has worked so hard on the book: thank you for your fresh ideas from the initial stages onwards, and for coping so calmly with the various changes, additions, alterations and panics. And finally, my sincere thanks go to designer Jane Hawkins, who has yet again done such a superb job of designing the book.

PICTURE ACKNOWLEDGEMENTS

Wholehearted thanks go, too, to all the people who have so kindly allowed Neville to take photographs of their premises and/or of their plants. The book would not have been the same without their generosity and our indebtedness to them all is listed below:

Mrs M Day, Fishtoft, Boston Lincolnshire: pages 29, 31 top left, 48;

Mr B Leggott, Boston, Lincolnshire: pages 113, 152;

Mr and Mrs R Oliver, Swineshead, Boston, Lincolnshire: pages 2, 17, 26;

Mr I Roberts, Benington Ings, Boston, Lincolnshire: pages 19, 24/25, 27, 30 right, 112.

BGI Conservatories, Birchgrove Garden Centre, Pinchbeck, Spalding, Lincolnshire for settings dressed with plants loaned by Mr and Mrs T Wilson of Plant Lovers' Nursery, Candlesby, Lincolnshire: title page, 4, 6, 7, 30 left, 56/57, 100 top left, 118;

Mr D Bowdery, Eau Brink Cacti, Kings Lynn, Norfolk: Contents page, 5, 10/11;

Mr and Mrs T Wilson of Plant Lovers' Nursery, Candlesby, Lincolnshire: pages 3, 78, 86 top right, 87 bottom right, 99, 134 bottom left, 135 top right, 136/137, 141, 142 right, 147, 151 (all).